Elite • 79

The Royal Navy 1939–45

Ian Sumner · Illustrated by Alix Baker

Series editor Martin Windrow

First published in Great Britain in 2001 by Osprey Publishing,
Elms Court, Chapel Way, Botley, Oxford OX2 9LP, United Kingdom.
Email:**info@ospreypublishing.com**

© 2001 Osprey Publishing Ltd.

ISBN 1 84176 195 8

Editor: Martin Windrow
Design: Ken Vail Graphic Design, Cambridge, UK
Index by Alan Rutter
Originated by Grasmere Digital Imaging, Leeds, UK
Printed in China through World Print Ltd

01 02 03 04 05 10 9 8 7 6 5 4 3 2 1

FOR A CATALOGUE OF ALL BOOKS PUBLISHED BY OSPREY
MILITARY AND AVIATION PLEASE CONTACT:
**The Marketing Manager, Osprey Publishing Ltd, PO Box 140,
Wellingborough, Northants NN8 4ZA, United Kingdom**
Email: **info@ospreydirect.co.uk**

**The Marketing Manager, Osprey Direct USA,
c/o Motorbooks International, PO Box 1
Osceola, WI 54020-0001, USA**
Email: **info@ospreydirectusa.com**

www.ospreypublishing.com

Acknowledgements

I would like to thank everyone who has helped me with this book,
especially my wife; Roy Wilson; the staff of the Royal Naval
Museum, particularly Dr Stephen Courtney; the staff of the Imperial
War Museum, and that of East Riding of Yorkshire Libraries.

Artist's Note

Readers may care to note that the original paintings from which the
colour plates in this book were prepared are available for private
sale. All reproduction copyright whatsoever is retained by the
Publishers. All enquiries should be addressed to:

Alix Baker, The Orchards, Forton, Andover, Hants SP11 6NN

The Publishers regret that they can enter into no correspondence
upon this matter.

THE ROYAL NAVY 1939–1945

THE ROYAL NAVY IN 1939

Britain, as an island nation, has always placed a great deal of faith in the Royal Navy as its protector against invasion. By the outbreak of the First World War, the 'Senior Service' had built up an unparalleled history and tradition, and appeared to be the largest and strongest navy in the world. After 1914, however, events combined to reveal serious problems, and flaws in ship design became disastrously evident in action against the German High Seas Fleet. Yet, for much of the succeeding inter-war period, the Government was unwilling to take action to rectify the situation.

This was partly a matter of economics, and the move to a peacetime economy. However, as the 1920s progressed, Britain committed herself to a number of diplomatic initiatives (the Washington Naval Treaty of 1921, the First London Naval Treaty of 1930, and the Anglo-German Naval Agreement of 1935) which limited the strength of the Royal Navy, both in terms of the total number of vessels in the Fleet by comparison with the other Great Powers, and in the size and power of individual new ship designs. These treaties meant that smaller navies were able to become almost as advanced as the Royal Navy and, in terms of the most modern ships, achieve parity with it. When these agreements were finally abandoned in 1936, and Britain was once again free to build new ships without restrictions, not even an extensive rebuilding programme could make up for lost time. When war broke out in September 1939, the Royal Navy found itself with a large number of ships of weak or obsolescent design.

When the long-delayed expansion eventually got under way in 1937–38, the form it took was conditioned by the attitude of the Admiralty towards the kind of war it expected to fight. Little had been learnt from the First World War. Although some of the technical faults which had bedevilled the design of capital ships – weak damage control, insufficient armour, poor shells – had been

Warrant Engineer Harry Longman wearing No.4 Frock Coat Dress. Longman was promoted to warrant rank in 1931, and served on HMS *Warspite*, HMNZS *Dunedin*, HMS *Pegasus*, and the aircraft carrier HMS *Glorious*; he lost his life when the *Glorious* was sunk by the *Scharnhorst* off Norway in spring 1940. Note the line of coloured cloth immediately below the 'distinction lace' of rank around his cuff; this is purple, to indicate that he served in the Engineering Branch.

LEFT **An Admiral's Inspection at the Boys' Training Establishment, HMS** *Ganges,* **before the outbreak of war. The inspecting admiral (right) and the commander of the base both wear No.1 Full Dress, complete with cocked hat, frock coat with heavily laced cuff patches, and sword. (RN Museum)**

BELOW **Harry Longman's wedding, with a guard of honour provided by other warrant engineers. The men wear No.3 Frock Coat Dress, which differed from No.4 only in the wearing of a cocked hat instead of a cap, and black shoes, as here, instead of white. Several of the men are veterans of the First World War, as shown by the 1914–15 Stars on view.**

corrected, Admiralty strategy remained wedded to the idea that the next naval war would be decided by a fleet action. The threat posed by the submarine had, it was thought, been conquered by the underwater sound detection system Asdic; while air power was believed to offer no serious threat because of the limited range of contemporary aircraft and the restricted capacity of the aircraft carrier. By 1945 the Admiralty had finally been disabused of these views, but its new-found knowledge was acquired with difficulty and only at the cost of many lives and ships.

The command structure

Control of the Navy was exercised through the Board of Admiralty, with political responsibility vested in the First Lord, a civilian, who was a cabinet minister. In 1939 the First Lord was Winston Churchill; when he became prime minister in 1940, his place at the Admiralty was taken by A.V. Alexander. Day-to-day administration was undertaken through five Sea Lords, all naval officers, each with a particular area of responsibility: the First Sea Lord acted as the Chief of Naval Staff, and was the professional head of the service. During wartime the Board, whose members were known collectively as the Lords Commissioners of the Admiralty, was also responsible for the control of merchant shipbuilding and repair.

A series of catastrophic coincidences in the late 1930s had deprived the navy, by death or illness, of a number of potentially excellent First Sea Lords, each of whom could have brought dynamic leadership to the post just at the time when it was most needed. The choice eventually fell on Admiral of the Fleet Sir Dudley Pound, who unfortunately was an officer of a centralising temperament, reluctant to delegate matters to the commanders on the spot. After Pound's death in 1943 the post went to the much more able Admiral Sir Andrew Cunningham, the former C-in-C Mediterranean.

At the outbreak of war, RN ships were distributed between a number of fleets and many bases, or 'stations', across the globe. In 1939 the principal battle fleets were the Home and the Mediterranean. In 1944, two more were created: the British Pacific Fleet, which served under American command as Task Force 57, and the East Indies Fleet, which operated in the Indian Ocean. Patrolling the seas in other parts of the globe was the responsibility of ships serving in one of the various stations: the America and West Indies Station for the western Atlantic and the eastern Pacific; the Africa Station for all waters surrounding that continent, except for the Mediterranean; the East Indies Station for the Indian Ocean; and the China Station for the western Pacific. At the outbreak of war, most of these stations had attached to them the equivalent of a squadron of cruisers and one or two battleships.

Home Waters, that is the seas around the British Isles, were divided into five commands, each further split into a number of sub-commands: Western Approaches (divided into Belfast, Liverpool, Milford Haven, Cardiff, Falmouth and Devonport); Portsmouth (Portland and Portsmouth); Nore (Dover, Nore, Harwich and Humber); Rosyth (Newcastle, Rosyth, Aberdeen, Stornoway and Clyde); and Orkneys and Shetland (which had only one sub-command, Scapa – but this was the permanent base of the Home Fleet).

Vice Admiral Bertram Ramsay, attending a Second Front conference 'somewhere in England', 1943. He is wearing No.5 Working Dress. Because of the wider lapels of the 'monkey jacket', any medal ribbons were worn higher and further out on the shoulder than on the tunics of the other services. As Flag Officer Dover in spring 1940, Ramsay commanded the Dunkirk evacuation. He became the Royal Navy's foremost expert in amphibious operations, holding senior commands for the invasions of French North Africa in 1942 and Sicily in 1943, before being appointed Allied naval C-in-C for the D-Day landings in Normandy. (IWM A14108)

Some extra commands were created during the course of the war. Dover was given enhanced status as a separate command because of its importance to the Channel approaches; Plymouth Command was created from Western Approaches; and, in 1945, a French and Belgian Coast Command was created for coastal forces. Extra sub-commands were also created in Western Approaches at Londonderry and Greenock. The number of vessels serving with each command changed throughout the course of the war. In 1939, they normally included at least one flotilla of destroyers (Western Approaches had four) and a squadron of older cruisers. The most modern vessels were invariably posted to the Home Fleet. As the war progressed, Western Approaches, responsible for the Atlantic convoys, naturally acquired a large number of escort vessels – in 1944, nine sloops, 104 frigates and 103 corvettes were based in its ports – while mine-sweepers and other coastal forces were concentrated along the eastern and southern coasts, particularly at Harwich, Granton and Plymouth.

The Royal Navy also controlled a number of shore establishments, including the three main naval depots – Devonport, Portsmouth and Chatham – as well as other training establishments. Since naval regulations insisted that each sailor was actually part of a ship's or boat's crew, these establishments were all given ship's names, and a craft with that name, even if it was no larger than a launch, was always to be found moored in a nearby harbour.

Three officers of HM Submarine *Osiris* in 1943: left to right, Sub-Lieutenants Colpoys and Rayner RN, and Midshipman Trevanion RNR – note the light blue 'turnbacks' or patches on the latter's collar, their colour identifying the Reserve. (IWM A18073)

Captain's Rounds on board the battleship HMS *Rodney*, 1943. The captain is in the background, but approaching the camera is the far more fearsome figure of the master-at-arms. The men are wearing No.6 Dress, prescribed for inspections and musters where No.1 Dress – the full dress uniform, which included gold wire badges – was not appropriate. (IWM A18523)

It must be appreciated that the Admiralty, unlike the War Office and the Air Ministry, was more than simply the administrative centre of the service. It also served as an operational headquarters, and could (and indeed frequently did) intervene in operations, giving orders to individual ships in all corners of the globe. Such interference could have far-reaching consequences for ships and men alike, as was the case with the ill-fated Arctic convoy PQ17 (see below).

THE ROYAL NAVY AT WAR

The battle for supremacy

If the Royal Navy was expecting to fight a fleet action on the outbreak of war, then it was to be disappointed. German tactics envisaged nothing of the kind and, indeed, the German fleet never put to sea as a body. Instead, the small number of German capital ships, the so-called 'pocket battleships', were sent out in ones and twos. Their orders were to harass and disrupt British merchant traffic and stretch the resources of the Royal Navy to the limit, while at the same time avoiding any direct confrontation with the enemy.

When they did meet British warships on the open sea, the restrictions imposed by their orders left the Germans unable to counter the aggressive ship-handling traditions of the Royal Navy, conferring on the latter a moral superiority sometimes vital to the outcome of individual actions. Thus, even as early as December 1939, three relatively weak

cruisers were able to take on the more powerful *Graf Spee*, and hound her into a position from which she could not escape. Despite her strength, Capt. Langsdorff preferred to scuttle his damaged ship, feeling it impossible to fight his way out of the situation

Yet in terms of their own limited objectives, the Germans did meet with some success. The Royal Navy had scarcely enough vessels to fulfil all of its convoy protection duties. Hunting down individual warships like the *Bismarck* was almost too difficult a task to perform on a regular basis. The sinking of the *Bismarck* in May 1941 was enormously important in terms of prestige and morale, but demanded an extraordinary effort, involving ships from both the Home and Mediterranean Fleets. Moreover, reluctant as they were to emerge and fight, the German pocket battleships retained the potential to wreak enormous havoc, and this in itself was sufficient to keep the Home Fleet pinned close to the British Isles, unable to take action to reinforce other theatres.

One key element in any success achieved by British ships was the introduction of radar. The first air warning sets had been installed in the battleship HMS *Rodney* and the cruiser HMS *Sheffield* in 1939, and from this small beginning the use of radar slowly spread throughout the Fleet. It was the use of radar aboard HMS *Suffolk* that allowed the British to keep track of the *Bismarck*, despite the poor weather conditions of the North Atlantic. The presence of radar on three of the Mediterranean Fleet ships gave its commander, Admiral Andrew Cunningham, an incalculable advantage over his Italian counterpart, whose vessels were not equipped with radar at all. The Type 279 sets in *Valiant*, *Formidable* and *Ajax* could pick up aircraft when still 50 miles distant, and surface vessels at rather closer ranges. In the action off Cape Matapan in March 1941, the British were able to concentrate against a section of the enemy fleet (the cruisers *Fiume*, *Zara* and *Pola*, and the destroyers *Gioberti*, *Oriani*, *Alfieri* and *Carducci*) without alerting the Italians to their presence, and then sink five of the seven (two destroyers escaped) in an exceptionally successful night-time action.

Yet, in comparison with the Germans and Americans, the Royal Navy was slow to exploit radar and other modern technology to their full potential; and its tactical superiority could sometimes be imperilled by its technical shortcomings. British gunnery direction was particularly under-developed. The Royal Navy did not make use of radar for gunnery ranging, preferring instead to rely on optical devices. The range and

According to the original caption, this picture shows the issue of the rum ration on board the battleship HMS *King George V*; but the rating second from the front of the queue has an HMS *Hood* cap tally, making this scene a poignant reminder of a ship's company who would soon die in the most dramatic single disaster suffered by the Navy during the war. One man from each mess is being given the ration for that mess. Two Royal Marines are doling out the grog (rum diluted with water at a ratio of 1:2); an officer and a PO look on. Most of the men are wearing their blue overall suits; note the 'non-substantive' badges of their speciality worn on the right sleeve on a white 'tombstone'-shaped backing. (IWM A1777)

bearing were obtained by viewing the target through a stereoscopic viewfinder, then using a mechanical computer, the 'Argo clock', to work out the correct bearing, allowing for the movement of the target and of the firing vessel. Using this method the director crew had to re-acquire the target after every change of course or change in deflection, by a system of flywheels, which were clumsy and of limited value in rough weather. The advantages conferred by gunnery ranged by radar soon became apparent. In the action against the *Bismarck*, the *Hood* was straddled by *Bismarck*'s second or third salvo; the *Prince of Wales*, her gunnery directors almost awash in heavy seas, took six salvoes to achieve the same degree of accuracy.

The relative backwardness of British gunnery direction was even more apparent in the area of anti-aircraft fire. In 1937, the Admiralty had opted for the High Angle Control System (HACS). This was an adaptation of the main gunnery control system, and was based on the odd assumption that enemy pilots would fly their aircraft at a constant height and speed and on a consistent course. This, unsurprisingly, proved not to be the case, and the system was not a success. Indeed, even in a pre-war anti-aircraft exercise, a radio-controlled target drone could fly over the Home Fleet for two-and-a-half hours without receiving a single hit, despite acting as the target for all the fleet's anti-aircraft guns. Once again, the German and American navies found a more sophisticated solution, the so-called tachymetric system, which used actual measurements taken from the behaviour of an incoming aircraft to predict its position. Nevertheless, perhaps because British industry was unable to manufacture the parts for a tachymetric system with sufficient precision, the HACS was used throughout the Navy for the duration of the war, and continued in service for some years after its end.

The band from the Training Establishment, HMS *Ganges*. Since the early years of the 20th century naval bands have usually been provided by the Royal Marines, but *Ganges* still maintained its own. Note the long canvas gaiters worn by all the members of the band; these were peculiar to the Navy. (Royal Naval Museum)

The final confrontation between a German pocket battleship and British ships took place in the Battle of the North Cape on 26 December 1943. The need to re-establish German prestige with a victory of any kind, following the defeat of Axis forces in the Kursk salient of the Russian Front, forced the fleet out of its tactical passivity. The *Scharnhorst* and her battle group of five destroyers (Z29, 30, 33, 34 and 38) were ordered to sea to intercept the next Russian convoy (JW55B). In gale force winds and heavy seas, the destroyers accompanying the *Scharnhorst* attempted to find the convoy but failed. The German commander, Admiral Bey, then ordered them home, hoping his bigger ship would better negotiate the stormy weather. But, thanks to good signals intelligence and radar, the convoy's escorts found the Germans first. Deprived of friendly intelligence as a result of poor co-operation with the Luftwaffe, and hampered by what seems to have been poor radar watch-keeping, the *Scharnhorst* blundered first into three cruisers – the *Belfast*, *Norfolk* and *Sheffield* – and then, turning away, ran headlong into the battleship *Duke of York*, accompanied by the cruiser *Jamaica*. It was radar-ranged gunnery which enabled the *Duke of York*'s first salvo to straddle the pocket battleship, while its second destroyed turrets and directors. Reduced to a helpless hulk, the German ship was finally sunk by torpedoes after a chase of two-and-a-half hours.

The cruiser HMS *Ajax*, seen from HMNZS *Achilles* in the South Atlantic, 1939. The *Leander* class cruisers were built under the restrictions of international treaties, and were undergunned when compared to their German and American contemporaries. Nevertheless, the aggressive way in which they and HMS *Exeter* were handled in action against the *Graf Spee* more than made up for deficiencies in firepower. (IWM HU205)

The battle for the convoys

Although attacks on British merchant ships by surface vessels and U-boats had formed an important element in German naval strategy during the First World War, the Admiralty did little to anticipate their reintroduction in any future conflict. There was, therefore, a severe shortage of escort vessels. Large 'Fleet' destroyers were thought much too valuable to be used in the role of escorting convoys, so a design based on a whale catcher was adopted – the 'Flower' Class corvette. Originally intended only as a coastal patrol boat, it was forced instead into the role of escorting long-range transatlantic convoys, bearing the brunt of the early years of the Battle of the Atlantic. It was a role to which the 'Flower' Class vessels were not entirely suited, as they were very small, slow (a maximum speed of 16 knots, slower than a submarine on the surface), and had a tendency to roll alarmingly in the slightest swell. The corvettes joined a motley collection of 'V' and 'W' Class destroyers of First World War vintage, and the barely seaworthy former American 'Town' Class ships. HMS *Campbeltown*, which was loaded with explosives and used to ram the dock gates at St. Nazaire in 1942, was one of this class; someone later commented that 'it was the best thing anyone could have done to the Town Class.'

These were later joined by a succession of purpose-built escorts: the 'River' and 'Castle' Class corvettes, which entered service from late 1942; the prefabricated 'Loch' Class frigates and their specialist anti-aircraft variant, the 'Bays' of 1944–45; and the 'Black Swan' Class sloops of 1942–43.

Convoy work remained fraught with difficulty throughout the war, especially in its early days. Escorts had to rely on visual sightings of German submarines, which was problematic enough in the North

Flags, official and unofficial.
(1) The White Ensign, flown by every Royal Navy ship.
(2) An admiral's flag, white with a red cross, which was flown only on his flagship (a vice admiral added a red disc to the upper corner nearest the hoist, a rear admiral a disc in both the upper and lower corners nearest the hoist).
(3) A 'Jolly Roger' flag was flown by every RN submarine on its return to port, marked with its tally of victories – this one belongs to the third highest scoring boat, HMS *Truant*. The bars represent ships sunk by torpedo, the stars, ships sunk by gunfire; all the decorations were in white, except for the first two bars, which were red, indicating warships.
(4) The 'Jolly Roger' of HMS *Tactician* – the middle bar of the three was red; this boat had also participated in 12 minelaying operations, an air-sea rescue operation (the lifebelt symbol), and five 'cloak-and-dagger' missions – this usually meant landing or picking up shore parties on enemy-occupied coasts.

Atlantic during daylight, but even worse at night, when the U-boats preferred to attack. A convoy of 45 ships, normally arranged in nine columns of five vessels, covered five square miles of sea. Shepherding such a group across the ocean during 1940–41 was the job of just four vessels, a destroyer and three corvettes. The escort's Asdic sets swept a 160-degree arc across their bows to a maximum range of 2,500 yards (but a practical range of only 1,200–1,500 yards). As well as searching for U-boats, the escorts had to try to keep the vessels together for the whole voyage, impressing upon them the dangers of making too much smoke or of straggling.

Radar once more provided the turning point of the campaign. The Type 279 sets, mentioned above, functioned well as aircraft warning radar, but were of little value for locating the low silhouette of a U-boat on the surface. This defect was remedied by the introduction of the Type 271 set, which operated on a different wavelength; this was capable of detecting a surfaced submarine at a range of up to 5,000 yards, and even a periscope at up to 1,500 yards. By the end of 1941, 100 corvettes had been equipped with the new device. This was allied with the introduction of 'Snowflake', a new illuminating round, much more powerful than the old star shells, which enabled surfaced submarines to be engaged at night.

The last known photograph of HMS *Hood*, taken from HMS *Prince of Wales* on 24 May 1941, before engaging the *Bismarck*. Minutes later, *Hood*'s after magazine was penetrated by a shell from the German pocket battleship and she blew up, sinking in three minutes with the loss of 1,416 lives – only three men were saved. The loss of the *Hood* was due in no small part to official parsimony in the inter-war period, which denied the ship a proper modernisation. The *Hood* was something of a national icon, and her loss was a blow to the country's morale which was only partly offset by the later sinking of her opponent. (IWM HU50190)

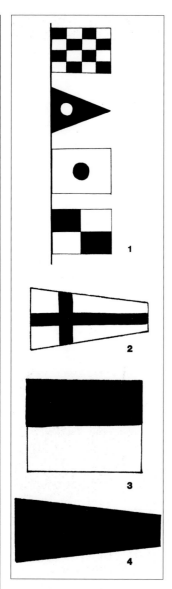

Although they were largely supplanted by Morse telegraphy and signal projectors, the navy still used signal flags.
(1) ZTH1, 'Prepare to go into action', as hoisted at the bombardment of Oran, 1940. The flags, from top to bottom, are blue/white; blue/white; black/yellow; and red/white.
(2) Pennant 3, 'Convoy is to scatter', as signalled to Convoy PQ17; red/white.
(3) Flag 5, 'Open fire – may be obeyed as soon as seen'; red/white.
(4) The black pennant flown by all ships engaged in attacking enemy submarines.

Asdic, however, was not quite the wonder weapon against submarines that the pre-war Admiralty had hoped. Contained in a radome under the ship's bows, it was vulnerable to heavy seas and, more importantly, it had several other serious operational drawbacks. The first of these was the German preference for attacking while surfaced, which rendered Asdic irrelevant. Secondly, Asdic could only establish the location of the submarine in two dimensions – it could not determine the submarine's depth. This presented problems when setting the exploding depth of the depth charges. Thirdly, the nature of the beam itself meant that contact with the submarine was lost after the beam had passed over it, at about 100–150 yards from the ship's bows. This was the 'dead time', which an experienced U-boat commander could use to dive or turn away from the approaching escort. The depth charge attack which followed so disturbed the water that it could be several minutes before contact was re-established.

A solution was found to the 'dead time' problem through the introduction, in late 1942, of forward-firing devices such as the spigot mortar weapon known as 'Hedgehog'. This consisted of 24 tubes, each of which fired a 65lb charge to a maximum range of some 230 yards. Hedgehog had the advantage of giving the U-boat captain no warning of an attack; its drawback, however, was that the charges only exploded when they hit something – a near miss had no effect at all. A heavier version, 'Squid', was introduced in 1944 after the Battle of the Atlantic had passed its crisis point. This weapon fired three charges of 350lbs each a distance of up to 700 yards. It was most successful during the short time it was in service, but its weight restricted its use to sloops and larger vessels – it was just too heavy for a corvette.

The great turning point came early in 1943, when centimetric radar, using very short wave impulses, enabled Allied ships – and, most importantly, aircraft – to track the smallest targets, day or night. This forced U-boats to spend much of their time submerged, where Asdic was able to locate them, and where their speed was much reduced. March 1943 was the last really bad month of the Battle of the Atlantic, with 108 ships totalling 627,000 tons lost. In May 1943 40 U-boats were sunk – 30 per cent of those at sea – and 37 in June. By late 1943 Allied monthly loses had been reduced to around 80,000 tons.

It was one thing to have powerful weapons; it was another matter entirely to make proper use of them. One of the first steps in this direction was the formation of Escort Groups, seven British (numbered B1 to B7) and five from the Royal Canadian Navy (C1 to C5). Each group was supposed to consist of nine ships – three destroyers and six corvettes – which served together as a permanent unit. Working regularly with the same ships improved the efficiency of the convoy escort, resulting in an increased number of successful U-boat 'kills'.

For new ships with new crews, however, some time was necessary to 'work up' the ship and crew, to get the ship's company pulling together as a team, and to make them familiar with their new vessel. In peacetime this process could last several months, but the pressures of wartime forced a drastic reduction, to a period of a mere two or three weeks. The dangers of sending a ship to sea on operations before it had been properly worked up were made clear during the hunt for the *Bismarck*, when a whole range of problems, including the jamming of the after main turret, became apparent on HMS *Prince of Wales* when she tried to come into action. Apart from mechanical teething troubles in a brand new ship, the members of the crew were simply not yet used to working together.

For smaller ships, working up was concentrated in particular locations. These were mostly to be found in Scotland, outside the range of German bombers – mine-sweepers in the Forth, Coastal Forces first at Portland and then at Fort William, and Combined Operations craft at Troon or Oban. However, perhaps the most famous of these working up bases was HMS *Western Isles*, set up in Tobermory on the island of Mull, for ships equipped for anti-submarine work – destroyers, frigates and corvettes. This establishment gave an excellent grounding in small ship handling; but more specialised anti-submarine work was undertaken at a number of Attack Teacher Houses, which were set up in the major ports. These were shore-based, and could therefore play only a limited role; however, this problem was resolved in 1943 with the creation of an establishment in Londonderry, based around the old yacht HMS *Philante*, which acted as a 'convoy' and was subject to mock attacks by a pair of older British submarines. This later became the Combined Services Anti-Submarine Training Centre, with the involvement of both the Fleet Air Arm and RAF Coastal Command.

The watches of the naval day	
Afternoon	Noon to 4 pm
First Dog	4 pm to 6 pm
Last Dog	6 pm to 8 pm
First	8 pm to midnight
Middle	Midnight to 4 am
Morning	4 am to 8 am
Forenoon	8 am to noon

A scene taken inside one of the 6-in turrets of the cruiser HMS *Orion*. A shell is rammed into the breech, while another one is prepared. The men are wearing working overalls and anti-flash hoods and gloves; in the right background, the petty officer has kept his cap on over his hood. (IWM A23468)

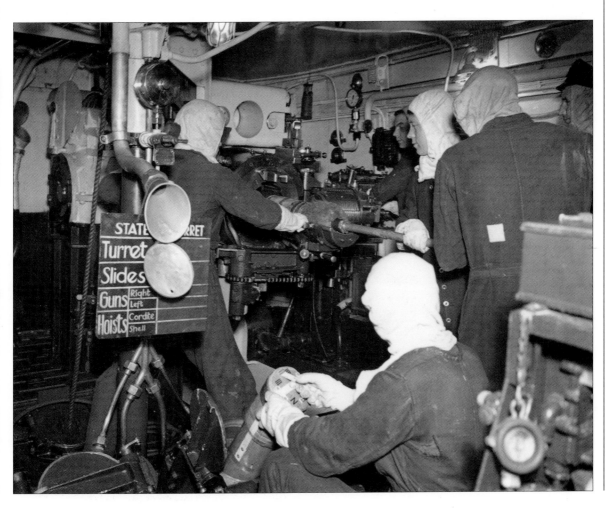

Successful as they were, the Escort Groups were still tied to the convoy; they could not leave it for long enough to hunt down a U-boat, particularly one in the hands of a skilful captain. This led to the creation of five Support Groups in March 1943. The strength of these units varied from group to group – perhaps the most famous, Capt. F.J. 'Johnny' Walker's 2nd Group, consisted of nine sloops (Walker flying his flag in HMS *Starling*). Two, the 3rd and the 4th, were composed of destroyers from the Home Fleet. Most significantly of all, the 5th, and then a new 6th, included an escort aircraft carrier. These groups existed as reinforcements for the convoy's close escort, but also had the opportunity to remain in one area to hunt submarines, rather than drive them away.

The first time Walker commanded a convoy escort (HG76 from Gibraltar to the UK in December 1941), his escorts sank four U-boats and shared a fifth with a Coastal Command aircraft. From that first successful experience, and from knowledge gained from a spell in command of the Anti-Submarine Warfare School, Walker developed a tactic of his own – the 'creeping attack'. Having located a U-boat, *Starling* stationed herself 1,000–1,500 yards distant, and then stalked her prey at a speed matching that of the enemy, sometimes as slow as two knots, making herself a sitting duck for any other submarine. The German captain would be aware that he was being stalked from the Asdic's tell-tale 'ping', but knew that the British ship was still over half a mile away. Walker then called up a second ship from his Group, which would pass by him, on the same course and speed, to disguise its approach. When the second escort reached a point just ahead of the U-boat, it released as many as 26 depth charges onto the submarine's predicted position.

Walker had the patience of a true hunter; the search would take as long as was necessary. In February 1944 the Group was called up to support the escort of homeward bound convoy SL147. *Starling* and two others sank U-238 after a hunt of almost three-and-a-half hours. At almost the same time, HM Ships *Kite* and *Magpie*, later aided by *Starling* and *Wild Goose* (all four were 'Black Swan' Class sloops), sank the particularly well-handled U-734 after chasing her for eight hours and firing 266 depth charges (a rate of consumption only made possible by replenishing

The Watch on Deck on board the *Scott* class destroyer HMS *Douglas* snatch a few moments for a hot drink on a cold, wet day; cocoa was popular. The ships of this class were all built in 1918, and were used for short-range escort work. Each man was issued with an oilskin coat for wear in bad weather – see Plate B3. Note at left the continued use of the ship's cap tally in place of the regulation 'H.M.S.' ribbon; and at right, the bow typically pulled round towards the front instead of being worn over the left ear as regulation. (RN Museum)

stocks from pre-placed stores carried on selected ships within the convoy). The Group sank a total of six enemy submarines that month with the loss of only one ship – another 'Black Swan', HMS *Woodpecker*, whose stern was blown off by an acoustic torpedo. Ultimately, the most serious casualty was Walker himself, killed in July 1944 by a stroke brought on by the pressures of the campaign in which he excelled.

The Arctic Convoys

The convoys carrying aid to the USSR via the north Russian ports presented the Royal Navy with an entirely different range of problems. Not only was the prevailing weather much worse, but the routes used by the convoys took them within easy range of German bombers stationed in northern Norway and, more significantly, within easy cruising distance of the remaining heavy units of the German Fleet. This threat shaped Admiralty thinking about convoy escorts, even though the Germans rarely came out from their anchorages. Such was the danger posed by the German ships that a major portion of the Home Fleet had to be committed to provide cover for the convoys to Murmansk and Archangel. The level of casualties was high particularly among cruisers and destroyers, let alone among the merchant ships themselves, and the tonnage transported to Russia in this way was relatively small compared

Even the official issue of bad weather clothing was not always sufficient for watchkeepers, as shown by this shot of the bridge of HMS *Inglefield*. (IWM A15401)

with the overland route through Persia; yet political pressure meant that the route could not be abandoned.

In reality, few convoys were actively threatened by German surface vessels. For one of them, however, the British reaction to the potential danger was to have the most disastrous of consequences. The interpretation of incomplete intelligence based on Ultra decrypts prompted the First Sea Lord, Sir Dudley Pound, to order Convoy PQ17 to scatter, as he believed that an enemy force led by the *Tirpitz* (one of the most powerful ships in the German Fleet) was at sea. The covering force of British cruisers had already withdrawn because of the threat of U-boats, and if the convoy had still been sailing as a body, its unprotected merchantmen would have provided easy pickings for the pocket battleship. Once they had scattered, however, they simply proved easy prey for the Luftwaffe and the U-boats: 23 out of 34 ships were lost. In fact, the *Tirpitz* and her consorts had sailed a day later than Pound had thought; even then they were quickly recalled, and never came near the route of the ill-fated convoy. This episode exemplified at their worst the consequences of the Admiralty's attempts to exercise direct control of an action from a distance.

Later convoys sailed with massive escorts. In September 1942 the 35 merchantmen of Convoy PQ18 sailed with a close escort of two destroyers, two anti-aircraft ships, two submarines, four corvettes, three

The appalling severity of the weather conditions faced by the Arctic convoys taking aid to north Russian ports can hardly be exaggerated. Here, a Visual Signaller on board HMS *Sheffield* tries to get his projector in working order. He is wearing a heavy coat, fleece-lined gloves, and a fleece cap over a balaclava. (IWM A6872)

minesweepers and four trawlers – much the same as that which accompanied the doomed PQ17. However, it was also shadowed by a Carrier Force comprising the escort carrier *Avenger* and two destroyers, and a Fighting Destroyer Force, which consisted of the light cruiser *Scylla* and 16 fleet destroyers. Added to this was a cruiser force of three vessels, and a distant covering force of two battleships (*Anson* and *Duke of York*) and the cruiser *Jamaica*. Against this show of power, the Germans could muster the *Tirpitz* (temporarily out of action with a mechanical problem), *Admiral Scheer*, *Hipper* and *Köln* and, more significantly in terms of their ultimate effectiveness, 20 U-boats. Seven of the convoy's ships were lost, all to U-boats or bombers, while Germany's surface ships remained in harbour.

When the Germans did make a sortie as, for example, against JW51B in December 1942, their leadership was once more timid; their attacks were not pressed home strongly and were easily beaten off by the convoy's covering forces. On that occasion the German force consisted of the pocket battleship *Lützow*, the cruiser *Hipper* and six destroyers. The convoy's close escort of destroyers, led by Capt. R. Sherbrooke in HMS *Onslow*, held off the attackers for almost an hour in a gallant and aggressive display of destroyer handling. The Germans withdrew when Sherbrooke's ships were reinforced by the cruisers HMS *Sheffield* and HMS *Jamaica*. In that engagement the German destroyer *Eckholdt* was sunk, and the *Hipper* so badly damaged that it never fought again. For his part in this Battle of the Barents Sea, Capt. Sherbrooke was awarded the Victoria Cross.

Depth charges explode astern. Depth charges were rolled off the stern and projected either side of the ship's beam in a number of pre-set patterns to maximise the volume of water covered. (IWM A4570)

Attempting to explode a mine by gunfire from a Lewis gun on board a Coastal Forces vessel. The heavy white roll-neck sweater became something of a 'trademark' of submariners, but was also popular with MTB crews. Note the lifejacket, which is a different pattern from that normally worn by ships' companies – cf Plate E1. (RN Museum)

The battle in the air

In 1918 the Royal Naval Air Service had been amalgamated with the Royal Flying Corps to form the Royal Air Force, thus depriving the navy of its own flying arm. Realising the value and power of aircraft at sea, the Admiralty pressed for the re-establishment of a naval air arm, fuelling a controversy which continued throughout the late 1920s and early 1930s. The RAF wanted to keep control of all military aviation, whether over sea or land. Indeed, it was prepared to push the argument much further. Moderate opinion within the RAF held that the development of the heavy bomber had rendered battleships all but obsolete; more extreme voices within the Air Ministry claimed that this would in fact be the fate of both the Army and the Royal Navy as a whole. The navy countered, arguing that air operations at sea had become so specialised that training, equipment and techniques had to become the responsibility of the Admiralty. It was the navy which won the day, and in 1937 the former Fleet Air Arm of the Royal Air Force was abolished in favour of the Air Branch of the Royal Navy, although the term Fleet Air Arm continued in unofficial use until its official adoption in 1953.

One effect of RAF dominance throughout the inter-war period, however, was that nothing had been done to develop a proper doctrine for the use of air power at sea. The role of aircraft was made subservient to the needs of the battle fleet, their duties restricted to scouting and observation. At the same time, there was little impetus from within the Admiralty to change this state of affairs and disrupt the primacy of the battleship. The role of the aircraft carrier was still largely defensive, to

OPPOSITE ABOVE 'Lucky Loo': a typical escort destroyer, HMS *Valorous*, seen here in Norwegian waters at the Liberation, 1945. *Valorous* was launched in 1917, but like others of her class was converted to an escort destroyer in 1942–43 by removing a boiler to make way for extra fuel bunkers, and by giving her an all-AA armament. Her nickname came from her pendant number. (IWM DOC521)

OPPOSITE BELOW A scene at the Western Approaches Tactical Unit. Three Wrens (left to right, a plotter, a leading Wren and a PO Wren) make out the positions of the convoy and escorts according to the instructions passed to them by the students, who sit behind the curtained partition in the rear.

The Women's Royal Naval Service had been disbanded in 1919, and as late as 1936 a committee reported that a Women's Reserve was unnecessary. In 1938, however, the WRNS was reformed – a decision which fortunately provided a nucleus of trained personnel on the outbreak of war. The initial intention was to recruit part-time volunteers from the relatives of naval personnel in the areas close to the three home ports – Portsmouth, Plymouth and Chatham. The first Wrens were trained only as clerical workers or drivers; but by the end of the war Wrens had served with distinction in almost all shore-based trades. At peak strength, in September 1944, there were 74,620 women in uniform. Wrens were not normally allowed to serve on board warships, although a few did serve afloat as cipher officers or coders on large transports. Nor were they given equality in rank with male naval officers and ratings; unlike members of the other two women's services, they were also subject to a different disciplinary code from male personnel. (IWM 27823)

provide air defence for the fleet. For this reason the new *Illustrious* Class ships (built 1939–44) were equipped with an armoured hangar, which ensured their survival in more than one encounter, but which restricted their carrying capacity to a mere 36 aircraft.

This apparent neglect of the air dimension reached the highest levels of the service. In December 1941 the former Deputy Chief of Naval Operations, Rear Admiral Phillips, decided to try to intercept a Japanese convoy bound for the invasion of Malaya, in spite of a complete lack of fighter cover, either naval or RAF. The action resulted in his death and the loss of both HMS *Prince of Wales* and HMS *Repulse* to Japanese aircraft off Malaya.

In one respect the Air Staff were correct: aircraft did constitute a real threat to maritime communications. The long hostile coast from the North Cape to the Dodecanese permitted German and Italian aircraft to intervene in naval operations, sometimes at great cost in terms of ships and lives lost – as experienced during the evacuations of Greece and Crete in 1941 – and sometimes simply in terms of resources. Such was the threat from the air that, during Operation 'Pedestal' in August 1942, a convoy of 14 merchant ships vital to the survival of Malta had to be escorted by as many as 44 warships, including three carriers.

In 1939, however, the Navy did not have aircraft of sufficiently high performance to carry out even the limited range of tasks they had been set. The special demands of operating over the open sea required an aircraft which could carry a variety of extra equipment, such as an arrester gear, a dinghy and an extra radio, and which had to have folding wings to allow practical numbers to be accommodated in a carrier's hangar deck. All these had an adverse effect on the weight of the aircraft, and thus on its performance. The restricted amount of space available on board a carrier also dictated the type of aircraft required. It needed to be able to undertake several roles, such as torpedo-bombing and reconnaissance – which meant that it was, almost inevitably, unable to excel in any of them.

When HMS *Eagle* entered the Mediterranean in 1940 she carried 18 Fairey Swordfish, and a mere three Sea Gladiators (without specialist pilots – they were flown by volunteer Swordfish pilots) to act as fighter cover. The Blackburn Skua dive-bomber was almost obsolete before the war began (although 15 Skuas did succeed in sinking the German cruiser *Königsberg* during an attack on Bergen harbour in 1940), as was its fighter equivalent, the Blackburn Roc. Deliveries of the Roc were so slow that the Admiralty was forced to place orders for a second type, the Fairey Fulmar, almost straight off the drawing board. As a stop-gap the Fulmar was quite effective, but it sacrificed speed to provide space for a second crew member. This did not matter in action against slower Italian aircraft, but the Fulmar came off second best against German types. The Swordfish biplane, such as those carried by the *Eagle*, was also in effect obsolete, but remarkably continued in service until the end of the war. It was an aircraft without any vices, manoeuvrable even at low speeds, and capable of carrying a wide range of loads, including radar.

Experience of using Hawker Hurricanes as catapult fighters prompted the introduction of another converted land-based type, the Supermarine Seafire. Although based on the pre-eminently successful Spitfire, the Seafire was totally unsuitable for deck landings because of

its long nose and delicate undercarriage. It is a measure of the skill and gallantry of naval air crews that even with this collection of ungainly and out-of-date aircraft, several notable successes were still achieved – for example, the sinking of the *Königsberg*, and the devastating raid by Swordfish from HMS *Illustrious* on Taranto in December 1940. However, it was not until a range of American types – the Martlet/Wildcat, Hellcat, Corsair and Avenger – all became available in large numbers that real success was achieved.

The development of the escort carrier was a most significant step in the struggle against the U-boat. In concept, the escort carrier was essentially a floating flight deck, with a small complement of fighters, designed to provide a continuous air umbrella over a convoy. The first ship of this type, HMS *Audacity*, converted from a captured German merchantman, entered service in late 1941, and was able to protect vital convoys by driving away the shadowing Fw 200 Kondor reconnaissance bombers. She was followed by nearly 40 others, all built in US yards. Frequently forming part of an Escort Group, they provided cover against enemy aircraft and, using aircraft equipped with ASV (Air-to-Surface-Vessel) radar, against enemy submarines as well.

It was the escort carriers which, together with the long-range Liberators of Coastal Command, closed the critical 'Air Gap' – that part of the mid-Atlantic which could not normally be reached by shore-based aircraft, where convoys had to survive without air protection. Speaking after the war, Admiral Dönitz recognised that increased coverage of the seas by Allied aircraft was one of the turning points in the Battle of the Atlantic.

It was the campaign in the Pacific in 1944–45 which finally killed the idea that the Fleet Air Arm could play only a defensive role. From the outset, the campaign presented severe operational difficulties. The ships involved had been sent out mostly for reasons of prestige, and were insufficient in number to make a real difference to the American campaign against the Japanese. The base of the British Pacific Fleet was in Sydney, Australia, too distant from the theatre of operations. An advanced base was therefore organised at Manus in the Solomon Islands, 11 days away by sea. Even then, the actual theatre of operations was almost as far distant again. The Royal Navy had developed ship types

The officers and men of HM Submarine *Stubborn*. On 11 February 1943, while in Norwegian waters, the submarine had been attacked by German destroyers which dropped 36 depth charges in 15 minutes, and forced the sub to seek refuge on the bottom – 200 feet *below* her test depth. After a nine-hour wait she eventually found her way home, under air escort. Clothing is a typically motley mixture; several men wear the white submariners' sweater. Some display an 'H.M. SUBMARINES' cap tally, and others the equally unofficial 'H.M. S/M'. (IWM A21954)

ABOVE **The venerable but ever-reliable Fairey Swordfish. Despite its low speed and open cockpit it was always popular with its crews. This 'Stringbag', L7675 '5G', served with 825 NAS aboard HMS Glorious. Note that the squadron code is also painted under the starboard upper wingtip. (IWM A3820)**

OPPOSITE ABOVE **The Blackburn Skua dive-bomber. Despite its success against the Königsberg, it soon found itself outclassed by enemy aircraft. This Skua, L2928 'S', was sent to 801 Naval Air Squadron, which embarked aboard HMS Glorious and HMS Ark Royal during the 1940 Norwegian campaign. Flying from Detling in Kent, it also fought in the skies over Dunkirk. (IWM HU2326)**

OPPOSITE BELOW **A Seafire, guided in by 'Bats', attempts to land on the carrier HMS Indomitable. The Deck Landing Control Officer, Lt Malcolm Brown, has painted his name in white across the back of his Irvin flying jacket, and also wears flying boots – cf Plate G3. (IWM EA7568A)**

based on ready access to a number of bases throughout the world, so all vessels had a limited range; they were not suitable for a long-distance campaign such as this, and had no organisation ready to back them up with supplies. The Fleet Train, a hurriedly assembled collection of naval and merchant ships both old and new, was unable to keep the Fleet in action for the full duration of the campaign.

Flying from fleet carriers (*Illustrious, Indefatigable, Indomitable* and *Victorious*), Fleet Air Arm squadrons equipped with a mixture of British and American types delivered decisive blows against Japanese shipping, but more especially against oil refineries in Sumatra. The strike against Palembang in January 1945, by Avengers from four different squadrons, severely depleted existing stocks of fuel oil for ships and aircraft and hit future manufacturing capacity. Between March and May raids were made against airfields and shipping in and around the islands of Formosa and Okinawa. It was here that the British practice of building carriers with steel decks and armoured hangars paid off, since they were largely proof against *kamikaze* attacks, in contrast to their wooden-decked US counterparts.

At the same time, ships of the East Indies Fleet were operating in the Indian Ocean in support of 14th Army's advances in Burma. The four escort carriers of the 21st Aircraft Carrier Squadron, and other detached carriers, launched strikes against Japanese shipping and airfields in Burma, Malaya, and the Nicobar and Andaman Islands. Their aircraft also provided the vital reconnaissance which led to the sinking of the cruiser *Haguro* by the 26th Destroyer Flotilla, led by HMS *Saumarez*, in May 1945. By VJ-Day, 16 escort carriers were serving with the East Indies Fleet. Carrier-borne aircraft were now able to project naval power on land as well as at sea, and the aircraft carrier quickly replaced the battleship as the true capital ship.

Aircraft handling parties (in the darker helmets), and fuelling and arming parties (white helmets) on the flight deck of the carrier **HMS** *Pursuer*. **The aircraft are Grumman Wildcat Vs of either 881 or 896 Naval Air Squadron.** (IWM A22363)

RECRUITMENT AND TRAINING

Royal Navy personnel fell into four categories according to their recruitment – Active Service, Royal Naval Reserve, Royal Naval Volunteer Reserve and Hostilities Only. The first was the pre-war, regular Royal Navy. The second, the RNR, contained some former Active Service officers and ratings who had volunteered to join after their discharge, but consisted mostly of serving Merchant Navy officers who completed one year's Royal Navy service before entering the reserves. All the members of the RNR were professional seamen who were recalled in wartime, and who therefore provided a useful reserve of trained men.

The third category, the RNVR, comprised landsmen who underwent periodic training at sea. Although, during peacetime, the RNVR consisted of both officers and ratings, from the outbreak of war all new entries were officers. Indeed, all officers who joined during wartime were posted into the RNVR, whatever their pre-war experience of the sea. As one contemporary, if rather cruel, saying had it, 'RNRs were sailors trying to become gentlemen and RNVRs were gentlemen trying to be officers'. In addition the RNVR also included a Supplementary Volunteer Reserve, composed of landsmen who liked 'messing about in boats' but who did not do any naval training. Two smaller volunteer reserve organisations existed in peacetime: the Royal Naval Auxiliary Sick Berth Reserve, and the Royal Naval Volunteer (Wireless) Reserve, formed from medical and radio specialists respectively, who undertook to serve in wartime but did no peacetime naval training.

Equivalent ranks – Royal Navy and WRNS

RN	WRNS
Rear Admiral	Chief Commander
Rear Admiral	Director WRNS
Commodore	Deputy Director
Captain	Superintendent
Commander	Chief Officer
Lieutenant-Commander	1st Officer
Lieutenant	2nd Officer
Sub-Lieutenant	3rd Officer
Midshipman / Cadet	Cadet
Chief Petty Officer	Chief Wren
Petty Officer	Petty Officer
Leading Seaman	Leading Wren
Able Seaman	Wren

The fourth and final category was that of Hostilities Only (HO) personnel, which consisted entirely of conscripted ratings. This split between wartime officers and ratings was underpinned by the idea that officers had always volunteered, whereas ratings had not, and therefore could not be described as such. In September 1939 there were just over 167,000 men in the Royal Navy; by the end of the war the total number of effectives had risen to nearly 710,000.

The officers

Active Service commissioned officers were trained at the Britannia Royal Naval College at Dartmouth. Most cadet entrants were aged 13 on entry, and followed a four-year course; however, a small number of cadets entered at 17 or 18, straight from school, under what was termed the Special Entry Scheme, and spent only one term at the College. Most of the senior career officers who served during the war had come through this system, although some of the older officers had also benefited from a preparatory spell at the Royal Naval College at Osborne on the Isle of Wight, which closed in 1919. The College at Dartmouth was evacuated in 1942 because of bomb damage, and from September of that year cadets were trained at HMS *Britannia* at Eaton Hall, near Chester.

The supply of Active Service and RNR officers was almost exhausted by 1942. From then on, the proportion of RNVR officers grew in importance until, by the end of the war, the Fleet was largely manned by

A group of Fleet Air Arm pilots on board HMS *Chaser*. Some are wearing No.5 Dress, others the battledress-like No.5A. Three are wearing Irvin jackets, and one has flying boots, but the others wear no special flying clothing apart from helmets and lifejackets – see Plate G2. (IWM A22353)

Handling parties on board HMS *Indefatigable* striking down Firefly Is of 1770 NAS into the hangars after a strike against Sumatra, 4 January 1945. The wings are being folded and braced on struts before they are moved onto the forward lift, which is at the 'down' position. (IWM A27167)

reserve officers (88 per cent of officer strength in 1945). No RNVR officer ever took operational command of a large modern warship, although a Captain RNVR did command the old, weak, minelayer HMS *Adventure*, while a Commander RNVR was appointed to the escort carrier HMS *Hunter* when she was acting as a troop carrier in November 1945. By then, however, Reserve officers were in command of 20 destroyers, some 50 corvettes and frigates, and a number of Fleet mine-sweepers. This stood in stark contrast to the situation during the First World War, when no Reserve officer commanded anything larger than a motor launch or trawler. To familiarise themselves with naval life, wartime entry RNVR officers spent perhaps their first three months as CW ratings (CW standing for the Commissions and Warrants Branch of the Admiralty). They were then posted to HMS *King Alfred*, in Hove, where they underwent a three-month officer training course before being commissioned as sub-lieutenants; an Active Service officer would have spent seven years as a cadet and midshipman to reach the same rank.

Promotion for all commissioned officers came automatically up to the rank of lieutenant-commander, but after that it was granted solely on merit. Promotion usually entailed a move to another ship.

Promotion from the lower deck in the pre-war navy was rare, and could only be obtained in the specialist branches, such as Engineering. Suitable Chief Petty Officers could be promoted to Warrant Officer – for example, as a Warrant Shipwright. Further promotion, based on length of service, was then possible to the rank of Commissioned Shipwright, the equivalent of a sub-lieutenant, and again to the ranks of Shipwright Lieutenant and Shipwright Commander. Promotion was, however, slow – ten years was the minimum period required at Warrant and again at

HOME WATERS, 1939
1: Captain, No.5 Dress
2: Master-at-Arms, No.3 Dress
3: Leading Seaman, No.1 Dress

A

WORKING DRESS
1: Lieutenant; Home Waters, 1941
2: Lieutenant, Royal Naval Reserve, non-regulation working dress; Home Waters, 1941
3: Signal Rating, oilskins; Coastal Waters, 1945

B

WORKING DRESS

1: Visual Signalman 3rd Class, No.3 Dress with jersey; Home Waters, 1939
2: Rating, working overalls; Home Waters, 1944
3: Rating, working dress; Coastal Waters, 1939

C

PROTECTIVE CLOTHING
1: Rating; Northern Waters, 1943
2: Lieutenant, Royal Naval Volunteer Reserve; Northern Waters, 1943
3: Rating; Northern Waters, 1945

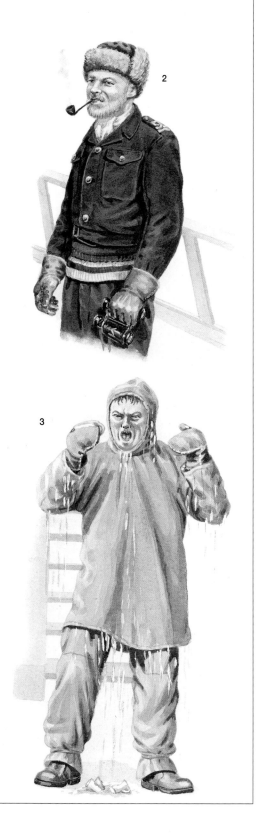

D

PROTECTIVE GEAR & WARTIME ECONOMY UNIFORM
1: Rating; Home Waters, 1942
2: Anti-Aircraft Rating 3rd Class; Home Waters, 1942
3: Petty Officer Anti-Aircraft Rating 1st Class; Home Waters, 1944

E

LANDING PARTIES

1: Leading Wireman, landing party; Home Waters, 1940
2: Leading Seaman, beach party, 'R' Royal Naval Commando; NW Europe, 1944
3: Lieutenant-Commander, RNVR, 30 Assault Unit; Germany, 1945

F

AIR BRANCH

1: Rating Pilot, Air Branch; Scotland, 1939
2: Lieutenant (A), Royal New Zealand Naval Volunteer
   Reserve; Home Waters, 1942
3: Aircraft direction personnel; HM aircraft carrier, 1945

G

WOMEN'S SERVICES
1: WRNS boat's crew; Home Waters, 1943
2: WRNS motor mechanic; Home Waters, 1943
3: Nursing Sister, QARNNS Reserve, ward uniform; RN hospital, 1942

H

FAR EAST
1: Rear Admiral; Far East, 1940
2: Petty Officer; Far East, 1940
3: Rating; Far East, 1945

FAR EAST
1: Lieutenant-Commander (A); Pacific, 1945
2: WRNS Chief Wireless Telegraphist; Far East, 1945
3: Surgeon Lieutenant-Commander, RNVR, No.14 Action Dress; Pacific, 1945

J

Rear Admiral Philip Vian comes aboard the submarine HMS *Torbay*, probably at Alexandria. The admiral and the staff officer just visible behind him are wearing the rather formal No.10 White Undress, while the submarine's officers are all wearing No.13 Tropical Dress – cf Plate I. (IWM A10277)

Commissioned status. This had caused some dissatisfaction in peacetime, since long-serving and experienced men were stuck in this rather rigid system, watching the midshipmen they had helped to train rise steadily up the promotion ladder. During wartime, however, many warrant officers were quickly promoted to the rank of full lieutenant.

Despite some opposition from individual senior officers, an increasing number of newly commissioned officers had to be drawn from the ranks as CW ratings. This system was accelerated in 1943, when it was realised that not even *King Alfred* could keep pace with the need for officers, and a selection programme was introduced in the main seaman training establishments.

From 1938, newly commissioned sub-lieutenants were asked to choose which branch of the service they wanted to enter. Many elected to join the Executive Branch, from which ship's commanders were drawn, but others preferred a more specialised role. Specialisation attracted extra pay, and many officers were drawn into submarines and aviation in this way. It could also provide access to accelerated promotion, compared to the 'salt horses' who remained in the executive branch. Those destined for specialist posts were sent on to a further training school, such as HMS *Mercury*, the Signals School in Hampshire, HMS *Vernon*, the Torpedo School at Brighton, the Navigation School at HMS *Dryad* at Southwick Park, or HMS *Daedalus*, for the Fleet Air Arm (see below).

Every ship was commanded by a commissioned officer. In the case of capital ships and destroyer flotilla leaders, he would normally hold the rank of captain; other destroyers were commanded by a commander or a lieutenant-commander, and escort vessels by a lieutenant.

Ships' companies (note that Royal Navy ships were manned by a 'company' and not a 'crew') were divided into Departments, according to specialisation. A capital ship, such as a battleship, might have nine such departments, each headed by a commander, lieutenant-commander or the equivalent. These would normally comprise the Commander's (which included the seamen), Gunnery, Torpedoes and Electrical, Navigation, Engineering, Medical, and Supply Departments, as well as the Royal Marines and the Chaplain. Each Head of Department had a number of immediate subordinates under his command. In 1944, for example, the Engineering Department of the battleship HMS *Nelson* had a commander (E) at its head (the letter E indicating a specialist engineer), supported by one lieutenant-commander (E), five lieutenants (E) and one temporary lieutenant; at the same time, the Medical Department was commanded by a temporary surgeon lieutenant-commander RNR with two surgeon lieutenants (one a dentist).

Manning to this level would be considered a luxury in smaller ships – in the same year, the 'S' Class destroyer HMS *Saumarez* had one commander (E), a surgeon lieutenant, a paymaster lieutenant in charge of supplies and a gunner (T) in charge of the torpedoes, but the remaining duties were split between six lieutenants and two sub-lieutenants. The 'Flower' Class corvette HMS *Saxifrage* had no commissioned or warrant Heads of Department – these posts were filled by petty officers.

Resupply at sea: HMS *Findhorn*, a 'River'-Class frigate, oiling from the escort carrier HMS *Shah*. This was a fairly new concept to the Royal Navy, and early attempts, like the one shown here, were performed by streaming a line astern. The Pacific War meant that new techniques had to be developed, including 'rassing' two or more ships abeam. (RN Museum)

The ratings

Adult Active Service ratings served an engagement of 12 years (previous service as a Boy did not count). All 12 years could be served with the fleet (so-called 'Continuous Service') or seven years with the fleet and five years with the reserves ('Short Service'). Before the outbreak of war, some 64 per cent of Active Service ratings had re-enlisted for a second term of ten years. Those due for discharge during wartime had their service extended to last until the end of hostilities. So, on the outbreak of war, the Royal Navy found itself able to draw on a considerable number of trained and experienced men; but this was soon to be diluted by wartime expansion.

On joining, all ratings, both Hostilities Only and Active Service, were allocated to one of the three manning depots. From there they were sent on to a new entry training establishment to learn the basics of naval life and routine – often HMS *Collingwood* at Fareham, or HMS *Royal Arthur*, in the holiday resort of Skegness (a 'ship' which, in 1941, the German propaganda broadcaster Lord Haw-Haw gleefully reported as having been sunk!). After this more specialised training might be undertaken, depending on the branch or trade of the seaman, either at one of the manning depots or at a specialists' school (for example, HMS *Duke* for

A beachmaster's HQ on the Normandy beaches, June 1944; all ranks wear khaki battledress, the officers with blue service caps. The officer on the left and the leading seaman in the foreground both wear Combined Operations flashes, on round and 'tombstone' backings respectively; both wear 'R.N. COMMANDO' shoulder titles – cf Plate F. (IWM A24092)

43

Another D-Day scene, aboard the command ship HMS *Largs* off Sword Beach. Left, Vice Admiral Bertram Ramsay, the Allied Naval Commander for Operation 'Neptune', the naval phase of the Normandy landings on 6 June 1944. Ramsay commanded 240 British and 85 US and other Allied warships and patrol craft; 4,126 landing ships and landing craft; 864 merchant ships, and 736 ancillary ships and craft – a total of 6,051 vessels, carrying more than 176,000 men and 21,000 vehicles. No other British sailor has ever commanded such a force; and probably no other at the time could have exercised the command with such complete success. Only Ramsay's early death in a plane crash in January 1945 robbed him of the wider fame he deserved as one of the architects of Allied victory. Ramsay wears Working Dress No.5A; centre is Rear Admiral Talbot, the commander of Force S, also wearing the BD-style uniform, together with an Army Royal Armoured Corps pattern steel helmet with his rank painted on the front, and the flash of 27th Armoured Brigade on the side – presumably a compliment from this element of the liberation army landed at 'Sword' by his command. At right is Air Vice Marshal Tedder, Gen. Eisenhower's Deputy Supreme Commander Allied Expeditionary Forces. (IWM A24020)

stokers, HMS *Excalibur* for communications specialists, or HMS *Gosling* for Fleet Air Arm personnel). Trained men were sent to newly commissioned ships as required, and remained on that ship until it was paid off – when it entered dock for major repairs or refit – or until it was scrapped. Seamen were rated as Ordinary Seamen until they were fully trained, when they became Able Seamen. Suitably qualified men could also go on to become Leading Seamen, then Petty Officers and Chief Petty Officers. Some positions on board ship also had particular titles – for example, the CPO in charge of signalling was known as the Chief Yeoman of Signals.

RNR ratings were enrolled from the Merchant Marine for a minimum engagement of five, and up to a maximum term of 25, years. Their annual training period was spent at sea on RN ships or in barracks. However, the take-up was not high, largely because men feared losing their civilian jobs whilst away at training; and the supervision of RNR ratings was sometimes rather casual.

Before the outbreak of the war RNVR ratings had been formed into administrative Divisions, each named after the principal river of the recruiting area, e.g. Mersey, Tyne, Humber, Forth. On mobilisation, a few days before the formal declaration of war, ratings were sent either to one of the manning depots or to a new entry establishment to receive naval training. It would appear that these men were often drafted together onto the same ships, although they could later be split up in the normal course of hostilities.

Boys were also allowed to join the Royal Navy, and many Active Service ratings had entered by this route. Entry was open to young men between $15^1/_2$ and $16^1/_2$ years of age, who were trained at one of three establishments: HMS *Ganges* at Shotley, near Ipswich, HMS *St. Vincent* in Gosport, and HMS *Caledonia* at Rosyth (a fourth, HMS *Impregnable* at Devonport, had closed in 1927). All of these establishments were evacuated at the outbreak of war, and boys' training was moved to HMS *St. George* on the Isle of Man, leaving HMS *Ganges* to train seamen ratings.

Boys also enlisted for a term of 12 years, which started only from the date of their transfer to the men's service at the age of 18. Two other avenues were also open to young men joining the navy. Under the Youth Entry Scheme, it was possible for those aged 17 to volunteer for naval service as an adult in advance of their call-up. Alternatively, youths between 15 and 16 years of age could take part in a competitive examination to win entry as an Artificer (a mechanic) or as an Air Apprentice.

A number of other organisations also came under Admiralty control during the war. Among these was the Royal Naval Patrol Service. This consisted of a large number of trawlers and their crews who were taken up by the navy in wartime. These men engaged to serve for the duration on their own vessel (and on that vessel only), wherever it might be sent; if they changed ship, then they signed a new agreement, unlike other naval personnel. The Minewatching Service, and riverine units such as the Clyde River Patrol, were made up of civilians in naval service, either part-time or full-time, engaged in patrol, mine-watching and boat work. Finally, the Special Repair Ratings (Dockyard) were civilian dockyard workers conscripted into the navy in order to provide dockyard facilities abroad. This had become necessary because the government's ability to direct manpower into the industries which needed it did not extend to the Colonies, several of which – for example Malta, Gibraltar and Ceylon – provided important dockyard facilities.

A 'Charioteer' – one of the first generation of British combat swimmers – wearing his Sladen suit, fitted with an oxygen breathing apparatus. Submarines were equipped with the self-contained Davis Sea Escape Apparatus designed simply to get a man to the surface; this was adapted for use with the rubber Sladen suit by Charioteers. Since the Sladen suit had weighted boots, however, it was unsuitable for frogmen. After research in experimental tanks at the Mine Warfare School at HMS *Vernon* and at the Naval Hospital at Haslar, both near Portsmouth, a new suit made from flexible rubberised stockingette was introduced. When worn with a breathing system that produced no bubbles, this proved ideal for the frogmen of those units who formed part of the Royal Marines. Another rubber suit was the so-called 'Ursula suit', named after the submarine where it had been developed. This was issued to the crews of some X-Craft. (IWM A22117)

SELECT BIBLIOGRAPHY

Those looking for an historical account of the Royal Navy during the war have a huge number of books to choose from, but should start with the three-volume Official History, *The War at Sea* by Captain S.W.Roskill (London, 1954-1961), and, for a more astringently critical view, Corelli Barnett's *Engage the Enemy More Closely* (London, 1991).

Uniforms

The most comprehensive history of naval dress remains that of Dudley Jarrett, *British Naval Dress* (London, 1960): it is, however, mostly concerned with the 18th and 19th centuries. The booklet *The Dress of the British Sailor* by Admiral Sir Gerald Dickens (London, 1977) is too short to be anything but a brief summary, but is well illustrated with prints and drawings, and does bring the story a little more up to date. Commander W.E.May's *The Dress of Naval Officers* (London, 1966) is the equivalent work on commissioned officers. The section by the same author within *Badges and Insignia of the British Armed Forces* (London, 1974) summarises changes in dress, with particular reference to distinction lace and other badges, and includes an extensive and authoritative list of non-substantive badges. The periodical *Mariner's Mirror* includes articles on dress from time to time. Naval Dress Regulations were published both separately and as an appendix to the Navy List.

HMS *Dolphin*, the submarine base at Gosport: Wrens wearing blue overalls handle torpedoes while the crew of submarine P556 look on. Under magnification the Wren in front on the left can be seen to wear the badge of a leading torpedoman on her right sleeve. (IWM A19471)

THE PLATES

NAVAL UNIFORMS

The specifics are described below under the various colour plates; a few words of introduction will suffice. The uniforms worn by the men of the Royal Navy had evolved in their own peculiar way. Although naval officers had worn a uniform since 1748, ratings had done so in the modern sense only since 1856. Thus, in contrast to the Army and the RAF, where officers' and other ranks' uniforms shared many basic similarities, in the Royal Navy they were completely different. It is also a measure of the conservatism within the service on matters of dress that a rating of 1856 did not look too dissimilar from a rating of 1939, or, for that matter, of 1956.

Naval dress was controlled by the Dress Regulations – on the outbreak of war, the 1937 edition. These could subsequently be amended by Admiralty Fleet Orders (AFOs), which are helpful in dating an official change in uniform. However, many changes occurred in practice only when supplies of an obsolete item had run out; further, difficulties of supply to more distant stations, such as those in the Pacific, meant that some months could elapse before new items were taken into use. At the same time, a certain amount of discretion was given to the Commanders of individual stations in deciding which garments could be worn on particular occasions – for example, tropical clothing, or clothing for night duties. Additionally, certain captains could relax regulations whilst at sea and out of sight of a senior officer, particularly on small ships such as corvettes.

Note that the titles given to the following figures – e.g. 'Home Waters, 1939' – refer to the provenance of the photographs used as main references; they do not imply that the clothing shown was necessarily particular to that place and date.

A: HOME WATERS, 1939
A1: Captain, No.5 Dress

Officers had twelve different orders of dress in 1939 – full dress, ball dress, frock coat with, and without, epaulettes, undress, mess dress, mess undress, white full dress, white undress, white mess dress, white mess undress, and tropical dress. Full dress, ball dress and the various frock coat orders were all put into abeyance at the outbreak of war. Dress for normal duties was this No.5, Undress, consisting of a double-breasted jacket ('monkey jacket'), trousers, cap and shoes. Originally introduced in 1889, the undress jacket covered the hips, and had two rows of four gilt buttons, all to button. There was a pocket in each skirt and one on the left breast. The cap was made of blue cloth, with a black mohair band and black patent leather chin strap; the peak was of

For inspections, every man had to lay out his kit in the fashion prescribed by regulations – as here by a rating named P.M.Collins serving on the cruiser HMS *Sheffield*. (RN Museum)

An officer's rank was indicated by a number of rings of gold distinction lace on the cuff of the jacket or the shoulder strap of the greatcoat, watch coat or tropical white shirt (see chart). On each collar midshipmen wore a white 'turnback' – a small rectangular patch with a button and a twist of white cord; cadets wore the button and twist only.

A2: Master-at-arms, No.3 Dress
For uniform purposes, ratings were divided into three classes: chief petty officers (Class I); petty officers and other ratings dressed as seamen (Class II); and all other petty officers and ratings (Class III). Classes I and III were dressed in broadly similar fashion (known as 'fore and aft rig'). There were ten numbered orders of dress for ratings. Working dress for all ordinary duties was No.3; its hot weather equivalent was No.5, and tropical rig was No.10.

Chief petty officers' No.3 dress was this double-breasted jacket, similar to that of the officers. The differences were the cloth used – CPOs wore navy blue serge – and the skirt pockets, which had flaps. Rank was indicated by three large (1in) gilt buttons on the cuff, in a line parallel with its edge. Trousers were blue serge, with a fly front. The cap crown, although slightly different in shape, resembled that of the officers; a white cover was likewise worn in Home Waters between 1 May and 30 September.

The department was shown by badges embroidered in gold thread and worn on each collar. This 'Jaunty' (from the French *gendarme* – the master-at-arms was the head of the ship's police) wore a badge consisting of a crown within a wreath.

A3: Leading Seaman, No.1 Dress
Class II ratings dressed as seamen included petty officers in the seaman, sailmaker, signal, telegraphist, photographer and stoker branches, with less than one year's service, and not confirmed in the rank; and all men and boys not otherwise included in Class III.

Class II ratings wore a uniform known as 'square rig', utterly unlike that described above: a cotton 'flannel', a jean collar, a jumper and trousers. The flannel resembled a modern T-shirt of white cotton, bound around the rectangular neck opening with a strip of 1/2 in wide blue jean (a denim-like cloth). Over this was worn the seaman's collar, made of blue jean, with three white tapes, each 3/8 in wide, sewn on by hand 1/8 in apart; it was secured by being fixed to the front of the trousers by a waistcoat-like arrangement. The next layer was the jumper – a single-piece garment, put on over the head. It was fitted to the body, with a vee-opening at the front coming to a point just below the breast bone; the bottom edge was in line with the crutch. The sleeves were fitted with cuffs, decorated with two small black ivory buttons. Worn under the collar, but over the front of the jumper, was the black silk handkerchief – an oblong scarf, 50in long x 12in wide, folded into a loop, knotted at the front, and secured to the jumper by black tape. (Despite popular tradition, it is not true that the three collar stripes commemorated Nelson's victories of the Nile, Copenhagen and Trafalgar, nor that the black handkerchief was a mourning scarf for the country's greatest sailor.) The trousers had a flap, rather than a fly, front: they were tightened by a lacing at the back of the waistband, and, by tradition, lacked pockets. The legs were cut 2in wider at the bottom than at the knee, giving the famous 'bell-bottomed' look. They were pressed with five creases across, rather than down, the legs.

Captain T.Pakenham RN of the sloop HMS *Black Swan* wears No.5 Undress, the officer's usual working dress for the first three years of the war – cf Plate A1. His ship was launched in 1939; like all its class, it was armed only with anti-aircraft and anti-submarine weapons. (IWM A15610)

blue cloth for the rank of commander and above, and of black patent leather for the rest. Flag officers (i.e. admirals of the fleet, admirals, vice- and rear admirals) and commodores 1st class were denoted by a double line of oakleaves embroidered in gold wire round the peak; for commodores 2nd class, captains and commanders, only the front of the peak was embroidered. In Home Waters, between 1 May and 30 September, the cap was worn with a white cotton cover (a provision abolished on the outbreak of war).

CW ratings undergoing training for a commission continued to wear their rating's uniform, but with a white ribbon instead of the cap tally.

One suit of jumper and trousers was kept for best (No.1 Dress, known as the 'tiddly suit') and one for working (No.3 Dress). In cool weather a blue crew-necked jersey was worn under the jumper. The two orders of dress could also be distinguished by their badges – of gold wire on No.1 Dress, and embroidered in red for No.3 Dress.

All Class II ratings wore a white knife lanyard attached to the waist and visible only at the neck of the jumper; attaching a knife was left to the discretion of the wearer.

Alone of the three services, full **beards** were permitted in the Royal Navy as a matter of routine, but moustaches alone were prohibited. Permission to 'stop shaving' was given by the rating's officer, whose permission also had to be obtained to resume.

Ratings of all three classes wore a number of **badges** on the sleeves of jacket, jumper or shirt. These were divided into three types – substantive, good conduct and non-substantive. Badges were usually sewn on to a piece of material of the same kind as the garment – cloth, serge, drill, etc. – before being affixed.

Substantive badges were those indicating rank or 'rating', and were worn on the left sleeve, e.g. that of this leading seaman is a single foul anchor. Boys under training had their own badges.

Good conduct badges were worn by all ratings except CPOs, and consisted of a maximum of three chevrons, point downwards, on the left sleeve, the top of the badge being placed 5in from the shoulder. One was awarded on completion of three years' good conduct (or 'undiscovered crime'...); a second after eight years, and a third after 13 years.

Non-substantive badges indicated the trade or speciality, and were worn by all ratings entitled to them. CPOs wore them on the collar of the jacket (see Plate A2), on the right cuff of the white tunic immediately above the centre gilt button, or on the right cuff of the overall suit. All other ratings wore them on the right arm, with the centre of the device midway between the point of the shoulder and the point of the elbow. These badges were not worn on overcoats, stokers' canvas jackets, tropical shirts or singlets. Exceptions to the rules about placement were made for the good shooting and diver's badges, which were both worn on the right cuff, 1½ in from the end of the sleeve. In Classes I and III, badges were placed on a backing cut to the shape of the collar; in Class II, they were mounted on a 'tombstone'-shaped backing (except for the six-pointed star of the Accountant Branch, which had a circular backing).

The badges were further graded by the addition of stars to show proficiency (which also brought an increase in pay), and/or a crown, indicating either an instructor or a rating deemed sufficiently able and well-qualified to take increased responsibility irrespective of seniority. These badges were too numerous to be listed here in full; 1939 Regulations include over 60 in addition to those worn by boys in training, and 1946 Regulations list 83.

There was little to distinguish the uniforms of ratings of the two **reserves**. Royal Naval Volunteer Reserve ratings were issued with a rectangular badge bearing 'R.N.V.R.', for wear on the left forearm; but many men removed it, trying to fit in with their Active Service messmates, and it was later banned by AFO 5643/42. RNVR ratings also had their own special cap tally bearing the name of their Division, e.g. 'RNVR (crowned anchor) HUMBER' (or 'Tyne', 'Mersey', etc.). Like

Every captain hoped for a good leavening of 'three badge men' amongst his crew for their experience and steadying influence. Leading Seaman George Griffiths, of the old destroyer HMS *Volunteer*, had seen 17 years' service, and wears his three good conduct stripes on his left sleeve below his rate badge. The badge on the right sleeve of his No.1 Dress identifies him as a gunnery rating. (IWM A22927)

Active Service tallies, these should have been replaced by 'H.M.S.' at the outbreak of war, but they continued to be worn until men were drafted aboard ship.

Ratings of the Royal Naval Reserve were not entitled to wear good conduct stripes; instead they wore good service stripes. These were awarded for service in the Reserve only, and could be superseded by good conduct stripes if these had later been earned after recall to active duty. Good service stripes resembled good conduct stripes but were narrower, only $3/8$ in wide. They were awarded for four, eight and twelve years' efficient service in the Reserve.

Boys wore the same uniform as adult ratings. Those in the Youth Entry scheme, who were serving as members of the Sea Cadets, Home Guard or Air Training Corps before their call-up, were permitted to wear a badge on their cadet uniform consisting of the letters 'RNYE' and a naval crown within a wreath.

B: WORKING DRESS
B1: Lieutenant; Home Waters, 1941
Shortage of materials made it impossible to continue producing uniforms to pre-war standards, and the uniforms

of all ranks underwent change and simplification during the war. For officers, economy measures principally affected the distinction lace. In 1939 the rings extended right round the wearer's cuff; in 1941 they were reduced to strips on the outside of the sleeve only; and in 1944 the material was changed from gold wire to woven braid. In the same year the cap badge began to be produced in die-struck metal rather than embroidered in gold and silver wire.

The sweater this officer wears was knitted from thick white wool; it was particularly popular on submarines, where it became an unofficial badge of that branch of the service, and in Coastal Forces. Note the thick white woollen stockings turned down over the tops of his seaboots; and the 'OOW' for 'Officer On Watch' painted on his steel helmet, which is finished in naval grey; the helmet was always to be worn when at action stations. A short painted section of rank distinction lace was sometimes seen on the helmet front. Working uniform worn at sea – especially in the smaller warships – often became discoloured and mildewed, with tarnished lace.

B2: Lieutenant, Royal Naval Reserve, non-regulation working dress; Home Waters, 1941

Officers belonging to the RNR and RNVR also wore rings of distinction lace, arranged in the same way as above, but different in shape. In the RNR, the wide lace was divided into two wavy lines each $3/8$ in wide and a maximum of $1/8$ in apart, and the curl was formed into a six-pointed star slightly overlapping the top stripe; the half-stripe was, however, a straight line. Midshipmen wore a blue turnback and twist, cadets a blue twist. Branch colour was worn in a single straight strip between the stripes, or as two strips placed on either side of the lieutenant-commander's half-stripe (see Plate J3).

Any form of working dress other than those mentioned above was strictly forbidden by the Admiralty, despite the rather formal nature of No.5 Dress which was impractical when working in small boats. However, disregarding these official prohibitions, a number of resourceful officers managed to obtain sets of Army battledress, and dyed them dark blue for use as working dress. This officer has acquired such a blouse and uses it with his naval trousers; he also chooses to wear a dark blue shirt.

Official opposition to the blouse uniform was short-lived; having banned the adaptation early in 1943 (AFO 1030/43), the Admiralty reversed its decision later that year, still forbidding use of the term 'battledress', but incorporating the clothing itself into Regulations as Dress No.5A, Working Dress (AFO 4669/433). The new uniform consisted of a serge blouse and trousers. The navy blue blouse had three gilt buttons down the front, one under the right lapel, and one on each of the two pockets. Rank was indicated on the shoulder straps. Trousers were also navy blue, with an extra pocket on the left thigh. The uniform was worn with boots, shoes or wellingtons. Working Dress was only to be worn on

board ship – officers were forbidden to wear it outside Naval Establishments or when on leave. The headgear was the usual peaked cap. There was no hot weather variant.

B3: Signal Rating, oilskins; Coastal Waters, 1945

Every man was provided with an oilskin raincoat, with the collar faced with black cloth, as part of his initial kit issue. The oilskin was heavy and unyielding, making movement difficult, and the coat was unpopular for any activity involving hard exercise. The cap had a chinstrap which consisted of a simple silk ribbon; this was normally kept folded up inside the cap until it was needed. One essential personal addition to foul weather gear was something to wear around the neck to stop cold water getting inside the clothing. All manner of towels and scarves were pressed into use; but they posed their own problems, since any build-up of salt crystals from spray blowing or breaking over the deck rubbed against the neck, causing extreme chafing and irritation.

C: WORKING DRESS

C1: Visual Signalman 3rd Class, No.3 Dress with jersey; Home Waters, 1939

Note the 'non-substantive' badge of his speciality and rate – crossed flags with a star above and below.

Each rating received only one free issue of clothing; he later had either to repair his uniform or buy replacement items from the ship's Supply Officer. The term 'slops' for clothing from this source, familiar from Nelson's navy, was still current. Ratings promoted to a rank entitling them to a Class I or III uniform would receive a free issue of that uniform when promoted.

A number of traditions had grown up in the pre-war navy around the wearing of the uniform, particularly that worn when going ashore. Many of these were passed on to the flood of HO ratings; most New Entries naturally wanted to

(1) **Officer's cap badge** – crown in gold and silver bullion wire and coloured threads with red velvet cushions, anchor silver, wreath gold wire for male officers and sky blue thread for WRNS officers, the whole on a black backing.

(2) **Chief Petty Officer** – crown and anchor as for officers, ring and wreath gold bullion wire; the metal version was all gilding metal.

(3) **Petty Officer** – as for CPOs but without wreath; the cloth version was embroidered in red. Chief Wrens and PO Wrens wore both badges wholly embroidered in sky blue.

(4) **Pilot's wings** – silver bullion wreath and anchor, the rest gold bullion.

(5) **Observer's wings** – wings gold bullion, the rest in silver bullion. A version in red on navy blue was worn on working dress.

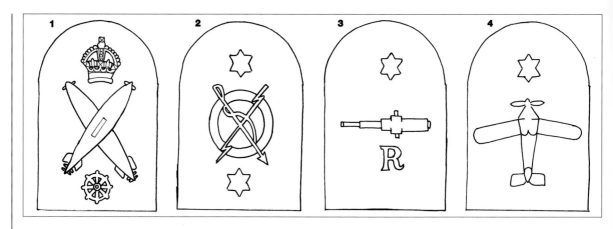

Four examples from the wide range of non-substantive badges:
(1) Torpedo Coxswain, worn by Coastal Forces.
(2) Higher Submarine Detector.
(3) Radar Control Rating 3rd Class.

(4) Air Gunner, 2nd Class.
This whole class of badges was worn on the right sleeve, in gold on blue, red on blue, or blue on white backing depending on the order of dress.

take on the appearance of the experienced 'staid hand' rather than looking like a newly joined 'sprog'.

The wire stiffening the cap was removed, and the edge reinforced instead with a line of stitching. The bow of the tally was made to keep its shape by sewing a small coin, usually a threepenny bit, inside; alternatively, the tally was cut short, its ends stitched together, and a larger, more complicated bow attached, made from a second ribbon. The cap was then worn placed right at the back of the head, with the bow over the left eye ('eye shooting'). The jean collar was washed repeatedly to give it a faded look, and was given a crease, traditionally by pressing it between the pages of the wearer's *Seamanship Manual*. A bib-like 'dickey', held taut by tapes around the body, replaced the 'flannel'. Finally, the trousers were pressed by being dampened and then folded in a bundle between two pieces of stiff card tied with a lanyard. Some ratings inserted cloth gussets down the seams to make the bell-bottoms even wider. All of this work was done by the rating himself, or by a skilled comrade. Traditionally, part of the naval week – usually Thursday afternoon – was set aside for the repair of clothing, when all hands were piped to 'Make and Mend'. Since seamen had embellished their best uniforms at least since the days of Nelson some informal alterations were winked at, but the more flamboyant changes brought down the wrath of authority. Eventually, private outfitters had to produce a form to confirm that any garment they sold conformed to Admiralty sealed patterns.

With the exception of clothing, nothing else in the way of personal equipment was issued to ratings: plates, knives and forks, mess tins ('fannies'), etc. were all part of the ship's stores. (This man carries a pannikin to collect his mess's rum ration.) All men had a large canvas kit bag for carrying their uniform, and a hammock. The 'ditty box', a small wooden chest for personal belongings issued to Active Service ratings, was replaced soon after the outbreak of war by a more utilitarian suitcase, made from green canvas strengthened with leather. Some ships, but by no means all, had lockers for personal stowage.

C2: Rating, working overalls; Home Waters, 1944
All Class II and some Class I and III ratings were also issued with a one- or two-piece blue overall suit. The two-piece suits consisted of a jacket with bib-and-braces trousers. Stoker ratings received two suits, but in coal-fired ships Class II stoker ratings instead wore the 'flannel' and fearnought trousers (fearnought was a thick woollen cloth designed to reduce the effects of flame). The overall suit was intended for dirty work, but was also worn by gun crews. In smaller ships, such as corvettes, it was virtually the normal working dress, as it was comfortable, and saved wear and tear on the No.3 uniform.

A white canvas uniform was also issued as a working dress, but this was rarely seen outside training establishments. It was similar to the blue uniform, but was worn with canvas gaiters.

C3: Rating, working dress; Coastal Waters, 1939
He wears the cap, jersey, working overall trousers – faded by frequent washing to a 'denim' shade – and sea boots with the tops turned down. Headgear for Class II ratings was the familiar sailor's cap. The crown was of blue cloth with an optional white cover, or of white duck. The diameter of the crown was $2\frac{1}{2}$ in greater than that of the band, which was also of blue cloth, and was covered by a black silk ribbon (the 'cap tally'), $1\frac{3}{16}$ in wide and 45in long. The tally was embroidered with the name of the ship in gold letters half an inch high, and tied off in a bow on the left side of the cap, the bow to be positioned over the wearer's left ear. Two changes were made immediately war broke out: the tally with the ship's name was replaced by one with 'H.M.S.' only, and the wearing of the white cap cover in Home Waters was abolished. Even so, many Active Service ratings continued to wear their ship's name – at least when out of sight of authority – and there were several unofficial variations to the regulation ribbon, including 'H.M. MINESWEEPER', 'H.M. SUBMARINE', 'H.M. DESTROYER', 'H.M. M.T.B.', and even 'H.M. X CRAFT'. The ribbon was shortened to 37in as an economy measure in 1940.

Crews of smaller vessels were sometimes less strict in their observance of Dress Regulations – particularly when, as is probably the case here, they were RNR serving on their own vessels. Neither the 'H.M. PATROL VESSELS' cap tally, the improvised scarf nor the ribbed-knit blue 'guernsey' sweater appear anywhere in the regulations. (IWM A2549)

D: PROTECTIVE CLOTHING
D1: Rating; Northern Waters, 1943
Apart from oilskins (see Plate B3), a wide range of other foul and cold weather gear was also available; this was not issued permanently to individuals, but only as required on board, and was to be handed in when the wearer went off duty. It was known as 'loan clothing', and included such garments as the frock sweater, the duffel coat and the Labrador smock. The duffel coat, as shown here, was made from heavy fawn or dark blue cloth. Loan clothing of this kind was issued to ships at a scale of up to 50 per cent of the ship's complement, enough for one Watch at a time. However, ships known to be proceeding to Northern Waters, which included all seas between Scotland and Russia, received loan clothing on an individual basis, as did those attached to Coastal Forces. This category also included a suit consisting of a fearnought jacket, trousers and gloves, issued as required to fire and damage control parties.
D2: Lieutenant, Royal Naval Volunteer Reserve; Northern Waters, 1943
Indeed, all manner of clothing could be pressed into service in an effort to stay warm while on watch. Captain Jack Broome, in his book *Convoy Is To Scatter* (London, 1972),

recalled: 'I was generally wearing two layers of silk underwear, socks and sawn-off socks as mittens ... My next layer was a pair of silk pyjamas, with a jumper – not button-up – on top. Then, vintage grey flannel bags, a uniform jacket which could have belonged to anyone's navy, and stolen RAF flying boots ... Once at sea my jacket usually gave place to a treasured submarine sweater [Broome had been a submariner in the 1930s], and sometimes a top layer of stolen RAF flying suit.' He continued:'A few [other officers] – presumably descendants of those Empire-builders who dressed for dinner in jungles – undressed and slept in pyjamas, between sheets ... [but] from the time I left my after cabin, clad for sea, until I returned to it X days later ... I never peeled beneath the outer silk pyjama layer.'

Everyone was issued with pyjamas (although certainly not made of silk), but they were rarely used for their intended purpose at sea. After a long period on watch, most men 'turned in' simply by taking off their boots, too tired to do much else. Instead, pyjamas more often provided an extra insulating layer for wear under the uniform.
D3: Rating; Northern Waters, 1945
The Labrador smock, introduced in 1945, was a hooded garment of green canvas, and came with trousers of the same; it was intended for use in windy rather than rainy conditions. The hood could be closed by a drawstring; the trouser cuffs were closed by an external tape.

Another innovation, which made its appearance late in the war was the 'goon suit' – a single-piece waterproof suit filled with kapok, making it light but very warm. The ships' companies of vessels serving in Arctic Waters were also issued with 'long johns' made from virgin wool, still containing the natural lanolin. 'When they got warm', recalled one veteran, 'you used to smell like an old sheep. Oh, terrible! I think most of the lads flogged 'em to the dockyard mateys in Belfast.'

E: PROTECTIVE GEAR & WARTIME ECONOMY UNIFORM
E1: Rating; Home Waters, 1942
During night-time watches and in wet weather, ratings were allowed to wear any old but respectable item as a replacement (or 'stepney') garment rather than spoil a good uniform. Men serving at Action Stations often took the laces out of their shoes, the easier to kick them off if they found themselves overboard.

Lifebelts were to be worn by all hands whenever there was a risk of damage – whether through enemy action or accident, at sea or in harbour, and in cold or temperate climes. In hot climates, belts were worn at the discretion of the senior officer, but if they were not donned then they had to be kept close at hand at all times. The lifebelt consisted of a wide belt, inflated by mouth, and two shoulder straps, all in blue cloth. Some officers continued to wear the Gieves design of First World War vintage – produced by the premier naval outfitter, it also contained a small flask of brandy 'for additional support'.
E2: Anti-Aircraft Rating 3rd Class; Home Waters, 1942
The standard Mk II steel helmet was painted grey; those worn by gun crews sometimes had the position of the wearer in the team painted in white. The helmet was frequently worn with the chin strap behind the head, to prevent injury from the effects of blast.

Another example of the way in which clothing regulations were relaxed in smaller ships. Here the men are wearing their overall suits, with shirts and pullovers in various combinations. Note the steel helmet with the number '2' painted on it, hanging in readiness on the gun in the background. These ratings have been taking advantage of a side effect of dropping depth charges – fish will be on the menu tonight. (RN Museum)

Gun crews, and those manning conning and director towers, also wore anti-flash gear (on loan) to protect as much bare skin as possible. This consisted of a hood, elasticated around the face, a mask, and a pair of long gloves elasticated at the wrist and elbow, all made from a fireproofed cotton material. All items had to be reproofed after a soaking. Anti-gas goggles were also used to protect the eyes, even though they had a tendency to mist up. Trousers were supposed to be tucked into socks, although photographs suggest that this may have been rare. Problems naturally arose in hot climates, where the normal shirt and shorts rig left large areas of flesh exposed; in these waters clean overalls had to be worn at action stations, despite the heat, until the eventual issue of No.8 Dress (see Plate J3). The issue of anti-flash gear was extended to all officers and men in sea-going ships in 1944.

Damage control parties were originally identified by distinctive brassards, which were replaced by large square badges in 1945. These used different colours to distinguish between the various parties: red for fire and repair (including magazine flooding and salvage pump parties), green for electrical, and yellow for pumping and flooding parties. Each badge was marked with a number between 1 and 5 to indicate the section, or with the letters 'HQ' for men attached to Damage Control Headquarters.

E3: Petty Officer Anti-Aircraft Rating 1st Class; Home Waters, 1944

For uniform purposes, Class III consisted of petty officers and men not 'dressed as seamen'. This included petty officers who had completed one year's service and were confirmed in the rank; regulating POs; sick berth POs and attendants; writer POs and writers; supply POs and supply assistants; engine room, electrical and ordnance artificers, 4th and 5th classes; armourers, blacksmiths, plumbers, painters, joiners and coopers; PO cooks, cooks and officers' cooks; PO stewards and stewards; and musicians.

Economy measures taken during the course of the war had their effect on the jackets worn by Class I and Class III ratings. New issues from 1943 onwards no longer included the cuff buttons (AFO 509/43); then, in the following year, a wool shortage resulted in the issue of single-breasted jackets instead of the double-breasted version required by regulations (AFO 154/44).

F: LANDING PARTIES

F1: Leading Wireman, landing party; Home Waters, 1940

Normal rig for shore parties and boarding parties consisted of No.3 Working Dress worn with high, laced webbing gaiters and 1908 pattern webbing equipment. Normal armament was the .303in SMLE rifle for ratings, and a Webley & Scott .455in revolver for officers. Officers could make use of the webbing Naval Pistol Equipment set, which consisted of belt, braces, pouch and holster, as well as a frog for a cutlass scabbard. It was only in 1936 that the cutlass had finally been relegated to ceremonial use, at least officially – but it certainly continued to be carried by some members of wartime boarding parties. The navy introduced its own versions of the Lee Enfield, but differences between these and the Army versions were almost wholly limited to modifications of the sights. Note this rating's non-substantive badge of a torpedo with a star above and 'L' below; wiremen installed and maintained specialist electrical equipment. The sharpshooter's crossed rifles badge was worn on the right cuff.

F2: Leading Seaman, beach party, 'R' Royal Naval Commando; NW Europe, 1944

Royal Naval Commandos provided beach parties capable of mounting small-scale offensive operations to secure the immediate area of a landing, and then to assist the Army in keeping landing forces moving swiftly across the beach. There were 22 Commandos, lettered from A to W (but excluding I); W Cdo was manned by the Royal Canadian Navy. Fully trained as commandos, first at HMS *Armadillo* at Ardentinny and then at the main commando depot at Spean Bridge, they participated in all amphibious landings from those in Madagascar in 1942 until the end of the war in Europe; the war in the Far East ended before RN Commandos could be deployed.

Their uniform was Army battledress with 'RN COMMANDO' cloth shoulder titles in white on dark blue. Below these the red-on-dark-blue Combined Operations flash was worn on both sleeves, originally in the 'tombstone' shape but later circular. Rate, good conduct and non-substantive badges proper were worn in the conventional positions, in red on dark blue backing. At the left shoulder a lanyard in a distinctive colour identified each unit – e.g. red for R (Roger) Cdo, old gold for H (Howe) Cdo, etc. Off duty the BD blouse was given a more naval look by being worn with the collar open revealing the 'flannel' beneath. Headgear was either the steel helmet or khaki knitted 'cap, comforter' (the green commando beret was never adopted); however, a photograph of some ratings of Roger Cdo shows them wearing seamens' caps with what appear to be khaki covers.

This man's weapon is the 9mm Lanchester sub-machine gun, a copy of the German Bergmann MP28/II produced in moderate numbers – and to pre-war quality standards – from 1940; increasing supplies of the US Thompson and later the British Sten led to most Lanchesters being issued to the Royal Navy. The Lanchester was distinguished by its full wooden SMLE-type stock, and the brass housing for its large 50-round box magazines. Special pouches had to be provided for the 1908, 1919 Naval and 1937 Pattern webbing sets to accommodate these. The Lanchester accepted the standard SMLE bayonet; its heavy stock also added to its hand-to-hand potential. It remained in RN service until the early 1960s.

A second type of unit active on invasion beaches was the Combined Operations Bombardment Unit. This was a combined RN/Royal Artillery unit providing Forward Observer teams for naval gunfire support. The RN contribution to these units was confined to wireless and visual signallers. Dress was conventional Army BD; ratings wore white-on-blue 'ROYAL NAVY' shoulder titles above the circular Combined Operations flash on both sleeves. Those who were parachute trained wore their wings between the right shoulder title and flash (although in RN No.1 rig wings were worn on the right forearm). Rank, good conduct and non-substantive badges were worn conventionally. The original headgear was a khaki 'cap, comforter', but at least one party replaced these with dark blue Italian berets, with the letters 'RN' in yellow-gold letters cut from Italian naval cap tallies.

F3: Lieutenant-Commander, RNVR, 30 Assault Unit; Germany, 1945

Naval officers serving ashore with Army units were permitted to wear khaki with a naval officer's cap in a khaki cover. The Dress Regulations, even in 1946, continued to specify a uniform similar to Army service dress, complete with Sam Browne belt and rank distinction lace of khaki braid on the cuffs; however, many naval officers, certainly in NW Europe, adopted Army BD with their rank displayed on navy blue shoulder straps. Officers taking part in landing or boarding parties simply wore Working Dress 5 or 5A with the trousers tucked into black leather gaiters.

30 Commando (renamed 30 Assault Unit in 1944) was a tri-service unit containing one section, No.36, composed wholly of RN personnel. They operated with Special Service forces and were trained particularly in intelligence gathering and in handling demolitions. Employed from Operation 'Torch' onwards, their missions frequently put them among, or even ahead of, the leading elements of invasion forces, with a view to securing useful enemy documents before they could be destroyed. Their transport consisted of jeeps, Morris scout cars and Staghound heavy armoured cars. Uniform consisted of Army BD with either a green beret bearing a naval cap badge or, more usually, the RN officer's cap with khaki cover, as illustrated. The shoulder title was 'ROYAL NAVY' in white on dark blue, above a pale blue '30' on a dark blue square, on both shoulders. Parachute-qualified personnel wore their wings between the number and the shoulder title on the right sleeve only. Some naval officers were also attached to No.33 Section, composed of Royal Marine personnel.

G: AIR BRANCH
G1: Rating Pilot, Air Branch; Scotland, 1939

Pre-war naval pilots were trained at No.1 Flying Training School at RAF Leuchars, and mechanics at the various RAF schools. Although the RNVR had been extended to include an Air Branch in 1938 the Royal Navy found it impossible to build up the necessary infrastructure of schools before the outbreak of war, so the RAF was still involved in training naval personnel, both aircrew and mechanics (although in decreasing numbers) for some years. This had the disadvantage that training was carried out only on RAF, and not Royal Navy, aircraft types.

The main depot for Naval Air Ratings was HMS *Daedalus* at Lee-on-Solent, with New Entry training at HMS *Medina* on the Isle of Wight; preliminary training for pilots was conducted at HMS *St.Vincent* at Gosport, with deck landing training at HMS *Condor* at Arbroath. Air Radio and Air Mechanics' training was provided at HMS *Drake* at Gosport, later dispersed to HMS *Cabot* in Bristol and HMS *Ariel* and *Gosling* near Warrington.

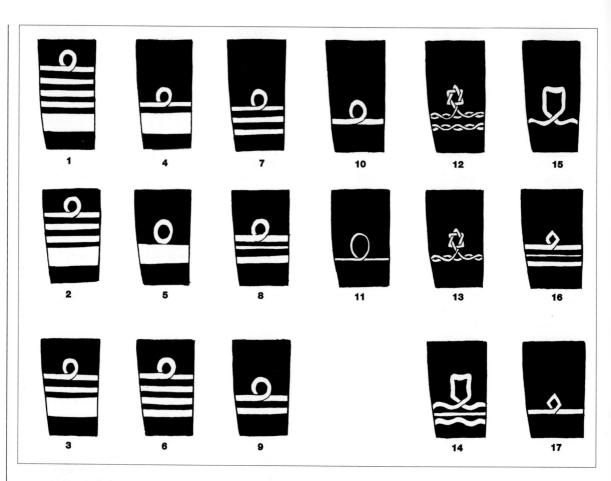

Officer's rank distinction lace: (1) Admiral of the Fleet, (2) Admiral, (3) Vice Admiral, (4) Rear Admiral, (5) Commodore, (6) Captain, (7) Commander, (8) Lieutenant-Commander, (9) Lieutenant, (10) Sub-Lieutenant, (11) Warrant Officer; (12) Lieutenant RNR, (13) Sub-Lieutenant RNR, (14) Lieutenant-Commander RNVR (the half-stripe was 'waved' like the others from 1943), (15) Sub-Lieutenant RNVR; (16) Third Officer WRNS, (17) First Officer WRNS.

Branch colours worn by RN officers

Engineer Officers	purple
Medical Officers	scarlet
Dental Officers	orange
Accountant Officers	white
Instructor Officers and Schoolmasters	light blue
Shipwright Officers	silver-grey
Wardmasters	maroon
Electrical Officers	dark green
Ordnance Officers	dark blue

Note: the Accountant Branch was renamed the Supply and Secretariat Branch in 1944.

The branch colours were worn occupying the whole area between the lines of distinction lace by officers of the rank of Lieutenant and above, or immediately below the stripe by Sub-Lieutenants and Warrant Officers.

RNR officers wore the colour in a narrow straight strip between the lines of wavy lace, or below a single line.

RNVR officers wore the colour occupying the whole area between the lines, or following the line of a single line.

In September 1939 the Air Branch consisted of 16 operational squadrons serving either at shore establishments or on one of five aircraft carriers; eleven catapult squadrons and one seaplane squadron, dispersed between 50 capital ships; and a further 11 second-line squadrons stationed either on shore or on one of two training carriers. By the end of the war it had increased to some 74 squadrons serving aboard 59 carriers of different kinds.

Given that the navy was forced to place so much reliance on the RAF for the training of its flight crews, it is hardly surprising that many wore RAF equipment and clothing. This man, from a photograph of one of the first courses for rating pilots held at West Freugh, Ayrshire (later the home of No.4 Observers' School), wears a 1930 Pattern flying suit with 1939 Pattern flying boots. His tally reveals that he remains on the books of HMS *Victory* at Portsmouth rather than the Fleet Air Arm depot, HMS *Daedalus*.

Air crew ratings did not have a special flying uniform until 1945, when Dress No.3A was introduced as working dress (AFO 1283/45). This consisted of a navy blue battledress suit with beret. Flying badges were worn on the left breast of the serge working dress; on other uniforms, including jumpers, they were worn on the left sleeve, $^1/_2$ in above the centre button (CPOs) or 1½ in from the point of the left cuff (other ratings). Some ratings wore an entirely unofficial 'FLEET AIR ARM' tally on their sailor's caps, replacing the regulation 'H.M.S.'. A beret with an 'H.M.S.' flash was introduced in 1945.

The Fleet Air Arm also included a number of Royal Marine pilots; for further details see Elite 57: *Royal Marines 1939–93*.

G2: Lieutenant (A), Royal New Zealand Naval Volunteer Reserve; Home Waters, 1942

Officers of the Air Branch wore conventional uniform but with the letter 'A', 1½ in high, inside the curl of their distinction lace. In addition, pilots wore their wings on the left sleeve, ½ in above the curl of their lace. Air Branch officers did not have a distinction colour. Officers and warrant officers who had qualified as Observers, whether from the Executive or the Air Branch, wore a distinction badge consisting of a silver foul anchor surrounded by a ring of silver rope in the shape of the letter 'O', crowned in gold, and set between two gold wings. Warrant officers who qualified as Air Gunners wore a similar badge but set within a ring of gold rope. Both of these badges were worn in the same position as the pilots' wings.

No.5B Working Dress for air crew officers was introduced only in 1945 (AFO 1283/45) – a battledress suit of navy blue serge, of air crew pattern, with the rank on the shoulder straps in the manner of sea officers. The headgear was the beret. The air crew pattern uniform differed from that provided for sea officers in a number of ways: the suit fastened up to the throat, it had a fly front, and the buttons on the pockets and cuffs were plain, without anchors.

Flying equipment followed RAF patterns for some time; this officer wears the Type B helmet, Mk IV goggles, Type D oxygen mask and 1941 Pattern Life Jacket Mk I. However, the Admiralty increasingly tried to develop its own – partly because they would be better adapted for shipboard use, but also to establish a separate identity for the Air Branch. Late in the war a number of AFOs were issued directing the greater use of the Types C and D flying helmets of 1944, the latter the tropical version, rather than RAF patterns. The principal flying suit for much of the war was the fleece-lined leather Irvin jacket and trousers. Whatever their disadvantages, pilots rejected alternatives which they thought might be too bulky in the restricted space of the cockpit. The first immersion suit, designed to keep the wearer both warm and afloat after crash-landing at sea, was introduced in 1943.

Commonwealth navies followed the RN's lead in terms of uniform, the main differences being in buttons and cap tallies. The tallies used by the five major Commonwealth navies were as follows: Australia, 'H.M.A.S.'; Canada, 'H.M.C.S.'; India, 'H.M.I.S.'; New Zealand, 'H.M.N.Z.S.'; and South Africa, 'S.(anchor)A.'. Unlike the Army and RAF, members of Colonial naval forces were forbidden to wear

A group of officers from one of the minesweeper flotillas based at Harwich. Note the different types of distinction lace: the lieutenant on the left, and the sub-lieutenant third from left, are Royal Navy; the 'sub' on the right is RNVR, and the others RNR. (IWM A10581)

shoulder titles bearing the name of their colony of origin. Dominion navies, however, were left to make their own regulations – e.g. New Zealand officers and ratings were permitted a white-on-black 'NEW ZEALAND' title when proceeding outside New Zealand waters in a RNZN ship, or when serving anywhere on an RN ship. The Royal Canadian Navy used similar titles.

It is impossible to do justice here to the uniforms worn by the men of all the Allied nations who manned ships in the UK and elsewhere after their own countries had been occupied by the Germans. As far as possible they tried to keep their own national uniforms, and at the very least retained their own badges and distinctions on RN issue items.

G3: Aircraft direction personnel; HM aircraft carrier, 1945
Flight deck personnel on RN aircraft carriers wore canvas recognition helmets similar in design to flying helmets, distinctively coloured for different parties: red and blue for the port and starboard watch aircraft handling parties (blue was changed to the more conventional green in 1944); white for servicing, fuelling and re-arming parties; and yellow for directing personnel, who also wore yellow jerkins and sometimes over-sleeves. The Deck Landing Control Officer (on HMS *Illustrious*, for example, he was a lieutenant-

commander) was responsible for ensuring that an aircraft about to land maintained the correct attitude and height. At the beginning of the war his instructions were regarded as advisory only, the main responsibility for a good landing falling on the pilot. The following year, however, it became obligatory to follow his instructions. He guided aircraft down with a pair of yellow 'table tennis bats' in the daytime (hence the universal nickname for the DLCO – 'Bats'), and a pair of illuminated Lucite wands at night.

In an effort to keep warm on the exposed flight deck this man has also managed to acquire an Irvin flying jacket and a pair of 1939 Pattern flying boots.

H: WOMEN'S SERVICES
H1: WRNS boat's crew; Home Waters, 1943
An increasing number of Wrens were employed in boat work, for which their standard uniform was unsuitable. It was therefore replaced by a shirt with a square neck similar to the men's flannel, and a blue crew-necked jersey. From 1941 onwards skirts were replaced by men's bell-bottomed trousers (complete with flap front). Boat's crews and Wrens employed in boom defence were permitted to wear the sailor's white lanyard and knife, and wore a watchcoat for

LEFT A leading Wren reports to a CPO Wren. Note that no two of these four wear the early type 'pudding-basin' hat in exactly the same way; and that of the girl at right has the tally 'H.M.S. *Drake*'. All Wrens are carrying gas mask cases, but the contours suggest that it is not just gas masks that are being carried. In the background is a naval sentry wearing a complete 08 webbing set and tall gaiters.

The first **WRNS officers' uniform** consisted of a double-breasted blue jacket with two rows of four gilt buttons (three to fasten), and two flapped pockets in the skirts; this was worn with a white blouse (officially a 'shirt') and black tie, a blue skirt, black stockings and laced shoes. Officers were permitted a *working dress* for temperate climes in 1944 (AFO 4584/44). This consisted of a serge BD-type blouse with shoulder straps, similar to that of male officers, worn with a rating's skirt or trousers (with two pockets and a side fastening, unlike men's trousers); the headgear was the beret with cap badge. Officer *ranks* were indicated by light blue distinction lace in three widths – 1¾ in, ½ in and ¼ in – with the men's 'curl' in the top stripe replaced by a diamond. The hat was a small blue tricorn with a black mohair band, and the badge of a crowned silver foul anchor within a light blue laurel wreath. Wren officer cadets wore a white band around their cap. The equivalent ranks in the Royal Navy and the WRNS are shown in the table on page 28. Female Medical Officers, however, were not part of the WRNS; they were considered to be members of the RNVR, and wore their gold wavy stripes with the red branch colour.

WRNS ratings wore a uniform similar to that of their officers: a jacket and skirt, a white 'shirt blouse' and black tie, black stockings (normally lisle, but rayon was preferred), and black leather shoes. Ratings' headgear until 1942 was a soft, brimmed 'pudding-basin' style hat (similar to the US 'Daisy May') made from gabardine cloth, with a black tally. Allegedly based on Bond Street fashion, it was loathed by everyone who had to wear it – not least because it was impossible to achieve any kind of uniform appearance – and for Wrens and Leading Wrens it was replaced by a cap based on the sailor's cap but omitting the metal stiffener in the crown. Both types of cap were to bear a tally of the 'usual pattern of the establishment' on whose books the rating was borne; but to judge from photographs, both the plain 'H.M.S.' and the establishment name were common. The sailor's cap was to be worn fairly well forward, and cocked either to the right (compulsory for parades) or to the left at an angle of not more than 15 degrees. In cold weather Wrens at first had to make do with a belted gabardine raincoat; this was supplemented from early 1940 by a double-breasted greatcoat.

Chief Petty Officer and Petty Officer Wrens replaced the gabardine hat with a tricorn similar to that worn by their officers, but of lesser quality until 1944, when the officer's pattern was adopted by all rates as the 'hat, tricorn, WRNS' (AFO 822/44, extended to tropical uniform by AFO 2796/44). However, CPOs and POs continued to wear a different cap badge: the former, a crowned foul anchor within a ring, the whole within a laurel wreath, all in light blue; the latter, similar but without the laurel wreath.

Wrens were not permitted to carry any kind of handbag or shoulder bag until an approved pattern was issued in 1944. Some compensation came in the form of a 'money belt' in dark blue (or white cloth for hot weather stations), with a white metal buckle, and a small pouch on the right-hand side fastened by two white metal press studs. Other banned articles included jewellery, umbrellas and coloured fingernails. Make-up, if worn, was not to be obvious to the onlooker. (IWM A1667)

---

cold weather – a garment similar to the greatcoat, but extending almost to the ankles.

Non-substantive badges were embroidered in light blue on a blue backing on the blue uniform. There was no system of added stars and crowns for WRNS badges. Wrens became eligible for good conduct stripes in 1945 (AFO 2425/45); the chevron used was identical to that of the men, but in blue. Qualifying service included time spent in the WRNS during the First World War, or in the Auxiliary Territorial Service, Women's Auxiliary Air Force, Voluntary Aid Detachments, or in a Dominion or Colonial navy during the Second World War.

Ratings attached to the Royal Marines wore naval uniform, but with the brass Royal Marines cap badge on a red tombstone-shaped backing on their sailor's cap.

H2: WRNS motor mechanic; Home Waters, 1943

Ratings performing certain duties received loan clothing; these included stewards, cooks, storekeepers, laundry maids and motor transport drivers. Wren mechanics, ordnance personnel and torpedo Wrens were issued with one of the two versions of the men's blue overall suit, as standard issue; here it is the two-piece version. Women's issues of the overalls were modified by the addition of a pocket, to hold pay- and identity books. These blue overalls were also issued for use in hot climates, but were eventually replaced by versions in khaki drill. Despatch riders were permitted breeches and black leggings, with either a soft peaked cap or a crash helmet. A duffel coat could also be worn. For dirty jobs, the white shirt was replaced by a version in dark blue. (See also MAA 357, *World War II Allied Women's Services*.)

H3: Nursing Sister, Queen Alexandra's Royal Naval Nursing Service Reserve, ward uniform; RN hospital, 1942

Although women had served in naval hospitals and hospital ships for centuries, female nurses were eventually re-introduced to the service in 1883 with a proper structure under the title of Naval Nursing Sisters, changed in honour of King Edward VII's queen in 1902. In 1939 the QARNNS had only around 200 nursing sisters plus some reservists; by the end of the war their number had risen to 7,000. They were employed largely in shore-based Naval Hospitals; the few that did serve aboard ship did so on transports.

The members of the service were all classed as officers and their uniforms reflected this, being based on those of the WRNS with two exceptions: rank was borne on epaulette

<table>
<tr><th colspan="2">Equivalent ranks –
WRNS and QARNNS</th></tr>
<tr><td>WRNS</td><td>QARNNS</td></tr>
</table>

WRNS	QARNNS
Commandant	Matron in Chief
Superintendent	Principal Matron
Chief Officer	Matron
First Officer	Superintending Sister
Second Officer	Senior Nursing Sister
Third Officer	Nursing Sister

QARNNS Rank Badges

Matron in Chief	Double gold border; black corded silk hat band, double gold top border
Principal Matron	Single gold border and gold bar; single gold top border beneath the cross and circle
Matron	Single gold border; single gold top border
Superintending Sister	Single red border; single red top border
Senior Nursing Sister	Red bar below the cross and circle; plain black mohair
Nursing Sister	No additions; plain black mohair

A QARNNS nursing sister in ward dress, in the imposing surroundings of the Naval Auxiliary Hospital at Cholmondeley Castle, 1942; cf Plate H3. Note the rating's cap, left; it still bears an HMS *Valiant* tally even though such tallies were officially abolished on the outbreak of war in September 1939.

Aboard ship nursing duties were carried out by Sick Berth Attendants (SBAs), whose medical training was undertaken at the naval hospital attached to each of the three manning depots. In peacetime this training had lasted from nine to 12 months, but under wartime conditions it was crammed into 10 weeks. The strength of the branch rose from 1,200 in September 1939 to 7,500 by 1943, of whom over 100 were officers (a warrant rank known as Wardmaster). SBAs served at all naval establishments, and on board all ships, including 11 hospital ships. Only one of the hospital ships, the *Maine IV*, was purpose-built; the remainder were requisitioned or captured merchant ships.

SBAs were Class III seamen for the purposes of dress, and wore a uniform similar to that of Petty Officers. They were distinguished by their non-substantive badge – a red cross on a white disc, with letters denoting specialisms below the disc. (IWM A11529)

straps instead of on the cuff; and the cap badge was different, consisting of the red letters 'AA' intertwined and superimposed on a gold foul anchor beneath a crown. The badges of rank were as the accompanying table.

The ward uniform of the QARNNS was designed by Queen Alexandra herself. It consisted of a dark blue dress with a full-length buttoned opening; over this was worn a white apron, detachable red cuffs, and a wide starched white collar. Over the whole was worn a short dark blue cape or 'tippet': nursing sisters had a line of red piping inset from the front and lower edges, more senior staff a broad red edge. The crown, anchor and cipher from the cap badge were repeated on the right-hand front corner of the tippet, placed above a red cross on a white circle edged in gold thread, all placed on a black rectangular backing. The veil was white with a naval crown embroidered in blue at the rear. The belt was of a silken material in dark blue or white, with a large white metal buckle similar in design to a naval officer's gilt sword belt buckle. This uniform was worn with black stockings and black shoes. The tropical version of the uniform was white, retaining the red cuffs and tippet piping.

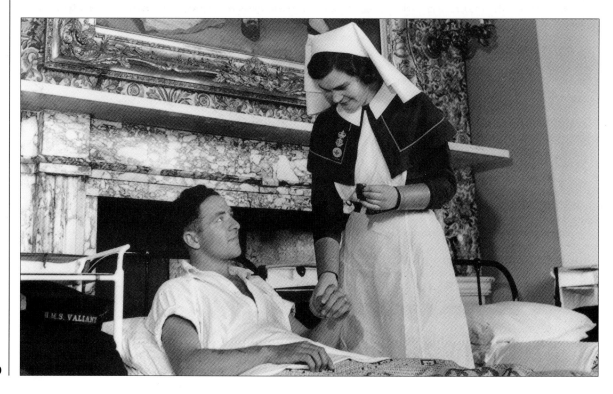

The Reserve of Nurses for QARNNS wore the same uniform but with silver instead of gold distinctions, and the word 'RESERVE' in silver wire below the cross and circle of the tippet badge and on the cap badge.

The uniform, even in its tropical version, was both impractical and uncomfortable on board ship; personnel on such duties were issued with a navy blue shirt and trousers, and a khaki version for tropical dress. Nursing sisters serving with the Air Evacuation Unit in the Far East wore the green poplin shirt and trousers of the Royal Australian Air Force Nursing Service, with unofficial brass badges in their slouch hats.

I: FAR EAST
I1: Rear Admiral; Far East, 1940
White Undress, No.10 Dress, was worn in 'Hot Climates'. The white single-breasted tunic was made of drill material, with five buttons, a stand-up collar, and two patch breast pockets. Trousers were plain white, worn with white shoes. The cap worn with this uniform was of the same pattern as that worn with the undress coat, but the crown was made from white cloth. Shoulder straps were made of blue cloth, except for flag officers of the Engineer, Medical and Accountant Branches, who wore straps of the appropriate distinction colour (see table, page 56), with the gold lace on top, and a leather backing.

I2: Petty Officer; Far East, 1940
In hot climates the blue jacket was replaced by a version in white drill; it was single-breasted (four buttons) and had a stand-up collar not more than 2in deep; there was a patch pocket on each side of the chest, but none in the skirts. Non-substantive badges were worn not on the collar, but 3in above the central gilt button on the right cuff (Class I ratings only – Class III ratings did not wear cuff buttons). This jacket was worn with white drill trousers and white shoes. It was exceptionally uncomfortable in hot weather, since the tightness of the collar frequently led to the wearer contracting 'prickly heat'. The white cotton tropical shirt and white drill shorts were therefore worn with increasing frequency as the war progressed. Badges were not worn on the shirt, and the wearer's rate could be indicated only by the cap badge. This dress was worn either with white socks and shoes, or with the rather more practical blue socks and black shoes.

I3: Rating; Far East, 1945
The white drill jumper worn in hot weather and known as No.5 Dress was intended to be looser fitting than the serge version, and was bound along the bottom edge with blue jean; the jean collar was integral with the garment. Trousers worn with this rig were either of white drill or duck, but were otherwise identical to the serge version. The rig was rarely worn as a working dress, however, and on most ships, even in the Mediterranean, ratings wore Tropical Dress, as shown here. This consisted of a cotton singlet in the same style as the flannel, and cotton drill shorts, worn with white socks and shoes, or blue socks and black shoes or boots.

J: FAR EAST
J1: Lieutenant-Commander (A); Pacific, 1945
For non-ceremonial occasions, and at the discretion of the Senior Naval Officer, Tropical Dress No.13 was permitted. The word 'tropical' could be interpreted rather loosely, and this became the standard working dress for all hot climates

Ratings from an un-named destroyer wearing No.10 Dress, off the coast of Malaya in 1945. Note the white 'flannels', the PO's white shirt, and the khaki shirt and shorts. In the uncropped photograph of the whole group no two men have exactly the same footwear – old shoes with and without laces, shoes with and without socks, and two different kinds of sandals. See Plates I & J. (IWM A25135)

including the Mediterranean. Tropical Dress consisted of a white shirt with shoulder straps, white shorts, white stockings and white shoes (or blue stockings and black shoes or boots), with a white cap. The Regulations also made provision for a Wolseley pattern sun helmet covered in white cloth, worn with a white *pagri* with a blue upper fold; this was discontinued during the war, and was replaced by the cap. Following the example of the US Navy, many officers in the Pacific Fleet adopted the more serviceable khaki in 1944–45; this received official approval in AFO 2423/45. The khaki aertex shirts (with long or cut-down sleeves) and the khaki drill shorts were usually of Indian manufacture, and could be worn with a matching khaki-crowned service cap. An alternative was a khaki aertex four-pocket bush jacket with integral cloth belt. The blue shoulder straps were sometimes replaced by khaki slip-ons with khaki braid ranking.

When in Tropical Dress, Air Branch officers wore their wings pinned on the left breast of the shirt above any medal ribbons.

J2: WRNS Chief Wireless Telegraphist; Far East, 1945
The first version of the white uniform for hot climates consisted of a short-sleeved dress with five gilt front buttons (later reduced to four as an economy measure). It had patch pockets on both sides of the skirt, and a separate,

Another Pacific Fleet group, of Fleet Air Arm pilots from 1771 NAS aboard the carrier HMS *Implacable*, July 1945. The pilots are all wearing the khaki drill uniforms adopted by officers in the Far East. Their rank is shown on shoulder straps (still with the letter A within the curl – second from right, front row). The man fourth from the left at the back wears the blue beret from Air Crew Working Dress – cf Plate J1. This attack squadron was equipped with the Firefly I. (IWM 29960)

buckle-less waist belt. This was replaced from 1942 by the separate blouse and skirt illustrated. The blouse was fastened by four white plastic buttons, but gilt ones were often substituted. The plain white skirt had a side fastening, with a concealed pocket. Headgear was a light grey or white felt hat for officers (and for CPO and PO Wrens from 1944), with a black mohair band and a cap badge; ratings wore a white version of the 'pudding-basin' cap until a version of the sailor's cap with a white cotton top was introduced. Officers displayed their rank on dark blue shoulder straps, POs on the points of the collar. Stockings and shoes were white. A solar topee was issued to some drafts for the Far East in 1941. At least one of these drafts made unofficial modifications to the uniform to make it more comfortable, including tailoring to improve the fit, omitting the collar button, shortening the skirt slightly, and wearing ankle socks instead of stockings (they earned themselves a rebuke for their pains). Flesh-coloured stockings were issued as a replacement for white in 1945.

From 1944, Wrens serving at RN Air Stations had their white uniform replaced in part by khaki items. These included issues of khaki bush shirts, khaki cellular cotton tropical shirts, khaki skirts, plus ankle socks and stockings which could be worn either with black leather shoes or white canvas shoes dyed with khaki blanco. Wrens serving at Air Stations in the Middle East also received battledress blouses and skirts for winter wear. In addition, those working on aircraft in the sun were loaned a khaki sun helmet. The khaki was more serviceable than the white, particularly for Wren Air Mechanics, and cooler than the blue overalls, but the white uniform had to be retained for ceremonial occasions. The initial issue of these items came from Army sources until supplies could be sent from the UK. Substantive and non-substantive badges were worn on the bush jacket and BD blouse, but not on the tropical shirt.

J3: Surgeon Lieutenant-Commander, RNVR, No.14 Action Dress; Pacific, 1945

In 1945 ratings were provided with a new Action Dress, No.8 (AFO 2126/45), following the introduction of a similar rig for officers. Intended to be proof against malarial mosquitoes and suitable for use in action, the new dress was also designed to replace overall suits and No.5 Dress. The shirt and trousers were identical in pattern to those of the officers, i.e. straight legged and fly fronted. Blue substantive badges were to be worn, but no others. To avoid delays, however, the first issues were supplied in a different dye and a different material from those intended. They came with the warning that 'they were not as effective against mosquitos ... and had worse laundering qualities'.

The version for Officers was No. 14 Action Dress, for wear at action stations when ordered by the senior officer. Its introduction was prompted by concerns that the existing rigs, particularly those worn in hot climates with short-sleeved shirts and shorts, provided inadequate protection against flash when in action, or against the malarial mosquito. The new rig consisted of a light blue shirt with shoulder straps, dark blue trousers and peaked cap, worn with shoes, boots or wellingtons. It was introduced in 1945 (AFO 2125/45), and priority was given to clothing the Pacific Fleet; but it is unlikely that mass issues were made before the end of the war (AFO 5261/45 records that supplies were available for general issue but is dated 13 September 1945). Ships' companies or individual officers proceeding from the UK to the Far East just before the end of the war may have worn the new uniform.

A medical officer served on every ship of cruiser size and above. Each destroyer flotilla had one medical officer and one sick berth attendant (SBA) aboard the flotilla leader, but the rest of the ships had only a coxswain with some first aid instruction. Other, smaller ships had either an SBA or someone with first aid knowledge. Submarines, in particular, were never allotted any kind of medical personnel. The situation eased slightly as the war progressed, but even in 1945 there were critical shortages of suitably qualified doctors. On entering the Royal Navy a doctor would undertake a six-month course on naval medicine, but this was reduced to a mere one or two weeks in wartime. The Admiralty were forced to institute a kind of apprentice system for new doctors, to ensure that they were fully conversant with the peculiarities of naval medicine, before they could attend patients.

Once aboard ship, doctors also found themselves acting as censor officer, and as codes and cipher officer. In action the doctor's post was at a Main Distributing Station, set up as a sick bay in a protected area of the ship; the SBAs and other first aid personnel were distributed at a number of first aid posts.

Non-executive officers (i.e. those not taking part in the command of the ship) were distinguished by the use of coloured velvet stripes placed between the rank stripes, below the single stripe, or, in the case of midshipmen and cadets, in a $1/8$ in wide stripe around the cuff. The colours of the various branches are shown in an accompanying table. Officers belonging to the RNVR used narrow distinction lace, $3/8$ in wide, in single wavy stripes; the curl had a rather squared-off appearance. The half-stripe of the lieutenant-commander was straight until August 1942, when it was waved following the line of the other stripes. Branch distinction cloth matched the line of the lace. RNVR midshipmen wore a maroon turnback and twist, RNVR cadets a maroon twist.

RNVR officers of the Special Duties Branch, which was responsible for electrical and electronic equipment, used emerald green as their distinction colour. This branch did not have a direct equivalent in the Royal Navy, where equipment of this kind was the responsibility of torpedo officers belonging to the Engineering Branch.

Four WRNS officers and one rating (second from right) wearing the white Tropical Dress, photographed at Algiers in 1943; cf Plate J2. (IWM A20133)

INDEX

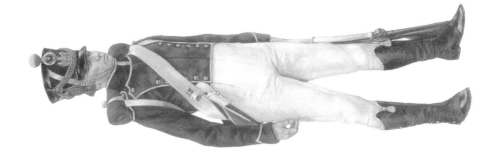

FIND OUT MORE ABOUT OSPREY

❏ Please send me a FREE trial issue
   of Osprey Military Journal

❏ Please send me the latest listing of Osprey's publications

❏ I would like to subscribe to Osprey's e-mail newsletter

Title/rank _____

Name _____

Address _____

_____

_____

Postcode/zip _____ state/country _____

e-mail _____

Which book did this card come from?

_____

❏ I am interested in military history

My preferred period of military history is _____

❏ I am interested in military aviation

My preferred period of military aviation is _____

I am interested in (please tick all that apply)

❏ general history   ❏ militaria   ❏ model making
❏ wargaming   ❏ re-enactment

Please send to:

USA & Canada: Osprey Direct USA, c/o Motorbooks
International, P.O. Box 1, 729 Prospect Avenue, Osceola,
WI 54020

UK, Europe and rest of world:
Osprey Direct UK, P.O. Box 140, Wellingborough, Northants,
NN8 2FA, United Kingdom

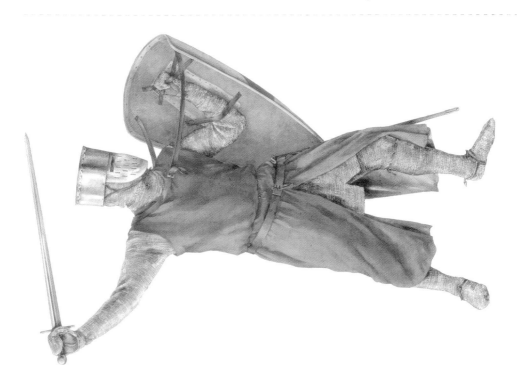

OSPREY
PUBLISHING

www.ospreypublishing.com

call our telephone hotline
for a free information pack

USA & Canada: 1-800-458-0454
UK, Europe and rest of world call:
+44 (0) 1933 443 863

Young Guardsman
Figure taken from *Warrior 22:
Imperial Guardsman 1799–1815*
Published by Osprey
Illustrated by Christa Hook

POSTCARD

Knight, c.1190
Figure taken from *Warrior 1: Norman Knight 950 – 1204AD*
Published by Osprey
Illustrated by Christa Hook

www.ospreypublishing.com